How I Taught My Brother To Cook

A Food Memoir and Guide to Simple Improvisational Cooking in the
Tuscan, Provençal, and American Peasant Traditions

John and Patrick Barrows

INKWATER
PRESS

Portland, Oregon

We dedicate this book to our mother, Helen Rose Napoleone Barrows, who passed away at age ninety-three, just as this book went to print.

Special thanks to Brian Timian, who did the layout and graphic design for this book; to our editor, Lindsay Burt; and to our wives, Debbie and Nancy Barrows – for their indulgence.

Contents

Foreword

John: This book is a collaboration between my bother Patrick and me. Since I'm the older and wiser brother, I would logically suggest that I am the better cook. In fact my grandson, Dylan, in a letter to me, proclaimed that I was "the bast cooc in the world". Who's to argue with that? Patrick, being the argumentative type, would probably disagree with that premise. In fact throughout this whole book, Patrick will argue until he's red in the face, that I am always doing and saying the wrong thing, or just being in general too fancy or cute. Patrick would suggest that "cooking is a study in earthy rustic-ness, and is not a fashion show". He would say that his teachings are more direct and blunt, while my methods are more politically correct. But I put up with it because I am after all the wiser, and already know that I am the better cook. So why debate these fine points? So, let Patrick harbor his opinions, deep in his craw.

But that's the point of writing this book. Opinions are like, well … everybody has one. There is no bible in the world of cooking. And this book doesn't remedy that problem. In fact, it is probably the cooking anti-bible. Because if there is one thing that Pat and I do agree on it's that cooking is a very personal experience, and no one person is more right than another. Though I hate to admit it.

So this book is dedicated to all those forebears in our family, and all of our other cooking gurus, who helped teach us the joys of cooking and eating, all in their own unique ways. And it is also dedicated to all of you who read this book, because our goal is to help you learn how to divorce yourself from the constricting act of following recipes word-for-word, to embrace your own culinary heritage, and to create and personalize your own cuisine.

Enjoy, if you can, our brotherly banter and our often diametrically opposed views on cooking. Learn from both of us. This book is about your becoming a better cook, in your own way, and enjoying it more. The main difference between you and say, Mario Batalli, is that he makes more money cooking (or babbling about cooking) than you, or Patrick and I, do.

Our style of cooking embraces what we might call the "Tuscan/ Provençal/American peasant" model. That is, one of simplicity, freshness, and healthfulness. So we often use, but not exclusively, a lot of culinary language that exudes from that food ethic. You may ultimately want to explore other cuisines, say for example your own ancestors' culinary roots, be they Chinese, Polish, Moroccan, Martian, or Venutian. . What Pat and I aim to impart here is a way of thinking about food and cooking. Not *what* to cook.

We finally dedicate this food and cooking diatribe to Tom and Ray Magliozzi, aka "The Tappit Brothers", the brotherly love model that we shamelessly use in our instructive methodology.

Introduction

John: As I've said before, I am the master cook of our cooking duo. But this is a story about how we *both* learned to cook well and enjoy eating. It's about growing up in a family whose roots are half traditional Yankee English, circa 17th century American immigrants, and half early 20th century Italian immigrants. It's about being lucky enough to have parents and grandparents, aunts and uncles, cousins, and brothers and sisters who all liked to cook and eat.

Patrick: The master cook?! Get a load of that one. I am not a psychiatrist, although I may need one, but Freud must have had something to say about self-exalting behavioral patterns. Anyway, as I recall, most of our family's specialty was the eating part. To be fair, each did have his or her few specialties that should not be forgotten. The two best cooks in our family were our grandfather, Giovanni Napoleone, and our great aunt Rose Barrows.

John: I'd add our Dad's sister, Aunt Betty, to that twosome. She was a sort of Bella Abzug of the kitchen. Big, brash, opinionated, and always the center of attention in the kitchen. Grampa and Aunt Rose represented the serious side of cooking. Betty was the vaudevillian. But whether we're talking about our dad's dirt farmer English antecedents, or our grampa, who came here as poor kid from Italy, it's about the fact that almost all immigrants who have ever washed up on America's shores were debilitatingly poor in their own countries, and came here not only for a better life, but to literally avoid starvation.

Patrick: The peasant food of yore has become the chic food of today. Not much different when I used to buy chicken wings because they were cheap, and that's what I could afford. Today, they are nearly priced up there with breasts. Chicken, that is.

John: Yeah, and food in fancy restaurants these days includes sweetbreads, kidneys, and tripe. But in the old world, food was often scarce, and it was never to be wasted, which is why offal like the heart, kidneys, liver, and brain was part of the diet. It was a function of what was available at various times of the year. Food was thus a central focus of people's lives. The procurement, cooking, and eating of food was a family thing, a community thing, and it was a religious thing, in every meaning of the word.

Patrick: Recipe creations today occur in a similar fashion in that when you have the skills you are able to pull a rabbit out of the hat even when the pantry seems empty. It's all about what you have on hand, and what are you going to do with it.

John: So this story is about cooking and eating in honor of our peasant traditions. It is about the fact that I take pride in the fact that I come from dirt-farmer stock on both sides of my family. And it is about rejuvenating the culture of peasants, before peasant was a pejorative term, before America became a nation of consummate consumers who want not only to keep up with the Joneses but indeed to *be* the Joneses. Before we all lusted for expensive designer kitchens, and got our recipes from lofty gourmet magazines. So, this is not a cookbook stuffed with recipes with every part spelled out to the smallest possible detail. Rather, this is more like a dialogue, or a way of thinking about doing some very basic things well, instead of cooking by following a recipe word-for-word. It's about thinking about what you're cooking. And it's about experimenting with and personalizing your cooking. And it's in the end about enjoying cooking and eating, even if what you cook isn't perfect. This is how I taught my little brother, Patrick, to cook. It'll work for you, too. Most of the time we don't even list the amounts of ingredients, or how long to cook something.

Patrick: Even if we do sometimes spell something out to the nth degree, it is for a specific and important reason, and not because you have to make something our way. For example, I absorb only that which has relevance to me, my style, and the food I prepare. I discard the politically correct cooking etiquette which Johnny tries to instill in me. If he and I owned restaurants, mine would be the hole in the wall with honest, straightforward good food in a casual setting. His would be the place with a stuffy maitre d'hotel, and squirt bottles for plating design. But he would still have good food if you don't mind dining in a "proper" atmosphere. So all things considered he teaches me more of what I do not want to do rather than how to do it. On the other hand, it's difficult to teach someone such as John as he listens with his mouth open. Therefore my efforts to teach him may be futile as he will continue "like a rolling stone, with no direction known" as Bob Dylan would describe it.

John: It's "no direction *home*". I don't deny that I often listen with my mouth open, though I'm working on that problem. If only Patrick would work on trying to prevent his brain from atrophying. It's people like him, who only see things in their simplest black or white forms, who are the guardians of the past. While it's my kind that is able to see the possibilities of the future. But it's that dedication to the old rituals that gives Patrick his confidence in the kitchen.

Patrick: I *am* totally confident in the kitchen and someday you will be, too, Johnny-boy. Now pay attention. In old Italy it is said, "The secret ingredient is the hand of the cook for it is the hand of the cook that expresses the heart". Sometimes on a hot summer day a drop of sweat may fall into the sauce, which is another secret ingredient. Like anything else, cooking takes practice, a lot of trial and error, and patience. Start slow. Start simple. Experiment. Never be embarrassed by anything that turns out bad. It's all about learning and feeling good about what you do, regardless of the level to which you want to take it. Remember, your best teacher is yourself. Books, even this one, are for ideas, not as bibles. This is true for the cooking shows one finds on television. If a recipe suits you, fine. If you want to modify or experiment with it a bit, by all means do so. But I suggest you have some experience under your belt before pulling "wonder if this would work" ideas out of your kiester. All cooking from the beginning of time meant trial and error, and it always will. By the way, this is how I taught *my* brother how to cook.

The Cooking Basics According to Us

The Kitchen Basics

Patrick: I am not by nature so simple a person, but my motto in life is "keep everything as simple as possible". This is no different for cooking. I prefer to shop for what I need on a daily, or every other day, basis. I prefer small general markets and specialty markets. Unfortunately, the "shops" of yesterday are giving way to monstrous super stores which may offer so called convenient one-stop shopping, but you are going to pay the price in quality, and in time, when all is said and done. Those big super markets are frustrating, annoying, crowded, and impersonal. Incidentally, one of those small markets I frequented almost on a daily basis was shut down, not by the want of the owner, but by the greed of the landlord to bring in a super chain pharmacy with deep pockets. Needless to say, the neighborhood was in an uproar, but the battle was lost again, for money speaks, and the chain game will continue to sweep the nation and world until all those little places are merely memories. There, I got that off my chest!

John: Patrick *will* get his shorts in a bunch when I talk about the food and shopping resources I have out here in the great Pacific Northwest. He's stuck in toney suburban Connecticut where everything, even the food, has to have a designer label. But he does the best he can with what he's got.

Patrick: My shorts are more like a knot than a bunch. But wait to see what happens to John when all his little shops get sucked into the Mega-Store Dante's Inferno, just as mine did. The unrelenting brat makes a point to boast of all of his fine shops whenever we speak. But keep in mind, it takes a person with great skills to create wonderful things with limited resources, unlike my uppity brother. That said, basically I only need a few things in order to create what I want.

> 🍽 *Functional kitchen layout. Kitchens are work areas, not showrooms. Things that do not provide a cooking purpose or function should be eliminated, especially within tight work spaces. Basically, get rid of the cutesy crap if it takes up space where a kitchen necessity can go. Most everything should be within easy reach or at most a couple of steps away. Whenever I work in someone else's kitchen, it usually gets me riled up. "Where is this?", "How can you cook with that?", "You live a life using stone knives and wearing bear skins", I say. But like the moral of this book, I make do not only with food on hand but with equipment available as well.*

John's chosen knives

- ***Cutlery that suits my needs.*** Never buy a set of cutlery. Buy one piece at a time until you have completed your arsenal. You only need what you will use. Do not buy a personality's name brand, but do buy from an established high quality manufacturer. I will not mention any manufacturer's names unless they want to pay me a fee first. You should know who the top manufacturers are. If not, buy the best carbon steel, forged steel you can afford. Do not buy knives with wooden handles! They will fall apart eventually.

Every pot you'll need

- **Cookware.** Same holds true as for cutlery above. Keep in mind that light weight cookware is light weight in performance. Difficult to control heat, they warp easy, and they are garbage. That is why they cost so little. Have at least one good 5 quart enameled cast iron Dutch oven in your arsenal.

- **Good butcher, farmers' market, and fish market.** Can be very difficult to find as time goes on and SUPER-MEGA markets gobble all the small places up, and in turn spit unknown quantities and quality at you. But you've already heard my gripes on this topic.
- **Food processor.** Only used for very fine chopping or pureeing. Let your knife chop whatever needs to be chopped.
- **Blender.** Use only when a whisk can't provide the speed and creamy depth needed.
- Food mill. The mill purees and removes unwanted pieces of whatever you are milling. Therefore you can't use a blender or processor instead of a mill.
- **Well stocked pantry.** Commonly used dried herbs, oils, and spices. Fresh herbs are used when you have them and when they suit what you're making. I don't know what dishes you will be preparing so I can't tell you what to stock. However, some no fail necessities may include; parsley, sage, rosemary, thyme, red pepper flakes, cinnamon, olive oil, canola oil, solid shortening, red wine vinegar, cider vinegar, brown sugar, baking soda, vanilla, corn starch, bread crumbs, beef broth and chicken broth. Each cuisine requires its own "pantry".
- **Pasta machine.** Top of the line, manual.
- **Pastry board.** Big enough to work on. At least 3 feet wide by 2 ½ feet deep.

Let's face it, the world is losing its June Cleavers at an alarming rate. If you are too young to know who June Cleaver was, then let me paint a quick picture. She was the epitome of the perfect housewife/homemaker as portrayed in the old sixties show, "Leave It To Beaver". Her job was to keep the house clean, shop, make sure the kids and husband were happy, and last but not least, to prepare the meals. While the feminists may have discounted this lifestyle as demeaning, it was a difficult job, required much time, not to mention sacrifice. It was very much taken for granted, and given less than due respect by others in the home. The lifestyle today has changed since then. The world economy has become extremely competitive forcing all but the fortunate to leave the house and get a paying job (where they can still be taken for granted and be under- appreciated) to meet the bills. This competitiveness has eliminated more than the homemaker. It is eliminating true quality in goods and lifestyle.

John: Patrick and I, due to unrelated and different circumstances, are in fact the "June Cleavers" of our respective households, even though we both still have non-homemaker careers and responsibilities. I think more and more families, and marriages have begun sharing the blended "June Cleaver/Father Knows Best" roles. The point, I think, that we are both making is that it isn't always easy to make food and cooking a priority anymore. But if you care about it, you'll figure it out. Oh, and you don't need a fancy enameled cast iron Dutch oven. A plain old, well-seasoned, cast iron one will do just fine.

Patrick: What a pain he is! He of all people should know that even though plain cast iron has its many benefits, it also has its drawbacks, such as cooking high acid foods, such as tomatoes.

Food Basics

John: Julia Child once described Americans as being "afraid of their food". For that matter we are excessively afraid of all things germ-like, or micro-scopic and alive. But that's another story. As I recall she was referring to our fear of eating fat, meat, eggs, cheese, carbs, butter, oil, dessert, or anything that might taste too good to be healthy for us.

> By the way, food can be healthful, but not healthy. Unless you eat while it's alive.

One of her examples is how we insist on pasteurizing cheese and keep it refrigerated. We want it dead. In Europe, cheese is "alive". It's essentially a way of storing milk so it doesn't sour. And by the way, cheese for this reason tastes better in France and Italy, for example. To my knowledge, more people die in the U.S. of gun shots, drunk drivers, and diabetes than Europeans die of "bad cheese". We are more intent on regulating cheese than guns, drunks, and fast food. In a *New York Times* Op-Ed I read just the other day, Peter Hoffman, a restaurateur, was quoted as saying:

"I am really dedicated to cooking by the seasons and supporting local agriculture …[if I could] buy a whole pig … I could put the hams in salt … then hang them to slowly dry for two years into prosciutto …and grind up the fatty shoulders with salt and pepper and stuff it into casings … and leave the sausages in a cool room for several weeks to naturally ferment … [but] I can't because the United States Department of Agriculture does not allow me to do that without refrigeration … This is astonishing because since Neolithic times, people have safely cured meats without refrigeration…So now Americans have to smuggle these foods home from Europe in their luggage."

John's Food Rule 1: Stop worrying about what you eat. Eat what you like within the parameters of a balanced diet, in moderation, and with good sense. Throw away the diet books, and listen to your body and your intuition. If you're going to die of something eventually, let it be by food. French and Italians eat well and refuse to die young, though they mainly do die driving like maniacs – and smoking. Yet unlike us they don't spend their 80's, 90's, and 100's living on *Lipitor* and a dozen other life-sustaining drugs, while being mistreated in nursing homes, suffering a quality of life that any sane person would not aspire too, just because they gained those extra 10 or 20 years working out obsessively and avoiding butter and pancetta.

Patrick: If you want to worry a lot about what you eat, then go ahead. And while you're at it, get plenty of exercise. But you know what? You can eat right, get exercise, and you'll die of something, anyway. All I'm saying is don't be a lazy glutton. Do what John says above and you will feel better for it in general. However, you don't know what cards you are going to be dealt in the future, so live life, within reason, while you still can.

John's Food Rule 2: Buy good ingredients. Unfortunately we can't always honor our peasant pasts by buying the cheapest food available. That's because here we have succeeded in mass-producing phosphate-laden, genetically modified food to lower its price. That's why we're fat as a culture. A couple of bucks can buy you a happy meal with a 64 ounce re-fillable Coke. If we want to eat really well (i.e. healthfully), we're forced to shop at stores and markets where food is sold that is grown rationally. Therefore it may cost you more. Buy a cheaper car that uses less gas, live in a smaller house whose mortgage is more reasonable, make your kids work to help pay for college, sew your own clothes if you have to, but buy some decent food! The single most important element in cooking and eating well is to start with good ingredients, and cook them simply.

Patrick: I agree, but don't fret over it if you can't afford the higher priced food. You will learn to make do when you need to with lesser quality ingredients. Just stay in tune with making your own stuff regardless if you have fresh farm organic asparagus or frozen. This is where creativity comes in. Working with what you've got, or can acquire.

John: Well, I'm not saying you absolutely must buy "higher priced food." In fact, as I say below, most people can wind up paying less for food and get higher quality, if they shop wisely and have an attitude that says for example, "I can get a better, more healthful piece of beef if I buy an organic shank, than if I buy a hormone-stuffed, feedlot-fed, mass-produced t-bone". And of course I am in favor of culinary creativity, especially if you can't find, or don't have, the ideal ingredient. I'm just arguing in favor of re-prioritizing your life, or more specifically your finances, so that you can afford better quality food if it's available, even if it means you can't afford to buy an SUV. What you put in your mouth is more important than where you park your butt for your commute to work, in my opinion.

John's Food Rule 3: Shop for bargains. In the meat department for example that means focusing on looking for the best of the cheapest cuts, like shanks (e.g. lamb, veal, beef – preferably from free-range, non-drugged, grass-fed animals, *if* you can find them). With a minimum of preparation, these cheaper cuts practically cook themselves perfectly every time, and are the most flavorful creations you'll ever eat. Plus you get to personalize your creations with your own preferences in herbs, spices, and cooking liquids. In the vegetable department shopping for bargains usually means buying locally and seasonally. The biggest mistake people make when planning a meal is to look through a recipe book, or see a recipe in *Food and Wine* or *Saveur,* for example, then go shopping for the required ingredients. Often the necessary ingredients are not in season and therefore not the freshest, not the most local, and not even easy to find at any price. The way to plan a menu is to go to the market, see what's fresh, local, and consequently the most abundant and cheapest, and think about what you can cook with them. Or just buy them and go home and figure it out.

Patrick: You know what? I don't have the time, or the markets here, to be searching out meat from animals that have been pampered like Cleopatra. My diet is varied enough that my consumption of one thing is not enough to kill me within the next 30 years. Of course, if I was a lab rat and forced to eat your average mega-store meat day in and day out, I would die quicker, while maybe pampered meat would have gained me an extra week. As far as by-the-book cooking, unless you absolutely *have* to make that oddball recipe that calls for things you may use twice in your life – well, that is your call. Sooner or later, you will learn that as your repertoire of food expands, and as you develop your own style, the ingredients you need will be pretty much on hand at all times. Of course, if you want to operate like a diner and be all things to all people, then you may need more than ingredients. You'll probably need psychoanalysis.

John's Food Rule 4: Treat your top-quality, local, fresh ingredients with respect. A two inch thick, grass-fed, well-marbled rib-eye cooked well-done and then slathered with A-1 sauce is a sacrilege. Fresh Northwest Coho wild salmon over-cooked, dried-out and covered with saucy concoctions that mask the poor fish's inherent subtlety is an abomination. If you like your steak well-done, then don't waste your money on a good piece of meat. Better yet, stop eating steak! It's an insult to the steer and a waste of your money. If you like over-cooked, dried out fish, buy salmon jerky. I saw a well-dressed suburbanite in my local market the other day trying to buy some rib-eye steaks (at $13.99 per pound) to make stew. The meat counter attendant ("butcher" in the old days) talked her into some nice shanks at $3.99 – and they were still hormone-free and grass-fed for that price.

Patrick: Good point here. However, if over-cooked steak is the way you like it, then go ahead. But if you do shell out the money for some really choice ingredients then you better take extra care on how you work with them. You wouldn't use your $1,000 alligator penny loafers to shovel manure in would you?

John's Food Rule 5: Eat slowly, with family and friends. Drink some wine. Talk about the food and other pleasant things. Don't be afraid of discussing how the dish could be improved. Eat in stages if you can, like the French who eat one dish at a time, so everything isn't all mushed together on your plate and on your palate. Always have a salad and eat it last, before your dessert if you have one.

Patrick: I guess if you are alone, you shouldn't eat. And I suppose the wine is so you can deal with your family and friends? Relax and enjoy, alone, or with others if you can. If you are on the run, do the best you can, but don't exchange potato chips for raw carrots, for example. By the way, Italians eat in courses as well. But there are many places, including the USA, that serve everything at one time, which isn't the end of the world unless you are one of those who pile their plates a foot high as if you are at an all-you-can-eat brunch because you think tomorrow will never come.

John: That brings up a point I've been meaning to make about how most Americans relate to their food. To most people here in this country quantity is the leading criteria for assessing value, when it comes to food especially. It's not uncommon to get this response when I ask an average American how he or she liked a restaurant. "It was great! The portions were huge!" So, it's not so much that those little piggies who pile their plates up are thinking that tomorrow will never come. It's more like, "The more I can pile on my plate, the more rewarding my dining experience." There's also this thing here in the States especially, that one has to eat a meal, just because it's mealtime, even if he or she is not hungry. It's just a habit, a Pavlovian response to the clock striking noon. I guess I just don't get the American obsession with needing to get more quantity for your money, in the food department. I'd rather eat one organic potato, which might cost 99 cents, than a half dozen chemical-laced mutant potatoes that cost $1.99 for a 10 pound bag. It's like shopping at Costco. You can buy all that stuff cheaply, so you can get it home and force it down your gullet. Where's the winning logic in that? The only diet that actually will help curb child obesity, the rise of diabetes, and other weighty issues, is to eat less.

John's Food Rule 6: I think this is a moral at the end of an Aesop's Fable. "Waste Not, Want Not". Save your pre-cooking meat and vegetable trimmings for making soup broths and cooking stocks. Save your leftovers for lunches and for ingredients to other dishes later in the week.

Patrick: Leftovers are one thing, scraps are another. If you have the space to save these scraps until you have enough to do something with, fine. If not, feed them to the dog, the pet rabbit, or the compost bin. Either way, the dog, or next year's garden, will thank you for it.

John: I would tend to think that throwing out the trimmings that you could use for stocks, has less to do with space than just not being bothered. Especially when you consider what good store-bought broths and stocks cost.

Patrick: I can't be bothered, OK!? Sue me. John, as you may have already noticed, is frugal to a fault. He used to be a panhandler on 42nd street, and at the end of the day, head to the Bowery to cook his organic road-kill over fires in 50 gallon oil drums. So you have to cut him a little slack, but just a little.

John's Food Rule 7: If your kids don't like everything that you cook, then they don't have to eat it. But don't get into a habit that wastes your time and is bad for them. That is, don't cook specially for them. They'll find something in your meal that they'll condescend to eat. And they won't starve to death until the next meal. There's nothing more to say about this rule. (I do have to add though that when I was a kid, I hated calves' liver, which my mother cooked at least twice a month. I ate some of the bacon that she had cooked to render the fat to sauté the liver in. Now I love liver, but my wife refuses to allow me to eat it. Fate!)

Patrick: I wonder if he has to get permission to go to the bathroom, too. As a kid, the peas, etc. went into my socks where they were later dumped into the toilet. If your kids are really talented they will be able to create an illusion of mostly eaten food simply by the careful rearranging of what they have on their plate while claiming they don't feel too well. By all means, don't make a separate meal for them unless you are accustomed to catering to their every whim in hopes of developing a spoiled brat. At worst, let them make their own meal. It's a start in the right direction for learning how to create food.

John's Final Food Rule: Always think about food. It's what sustains our bodies, hence our minds and our spirits. If you respect your food, then it means you respect yourself. And of course vice versa.

Patrick: I gotta say I think of other things besides food. But I think I understand what John is saying. When working with food, think food. Same thing goes for sex. When having sex, don't think about food, unless of course you use certain foods as part of your sexual exploits.

John: Even then you shouldn't be thinking about the food.

Patrick: Here's *my* final food rule. "You can fool some of the people all of the time, and all of the people some of the time, but you cannot fool all of the people all of the time". I think Abe Lincoln said that. The point here is not about fooling people but pleasing them. You need to cook to please *your* taste, first and foremost. Not everyone is going to like everything you make because everyone has his own taste buds. This is why so many different varieties of bagels are made. If you know the preparation has come out the way you wanted it, then it's the way it should be. If it did not, then by all means accept comments from others. When cooking for people other than your family, whose tastes you know, then you need to maybe plan a somewhat "benign" meal, or something that will probably please most of the people. In other words, figure that most people are accustomed to basic tastes and do not try to get too cute. You may just be wasting your time and food. For example, make cheese ravioli instead of pumpkin ravioli, or grilled shrimp instead of sautéed squid, and *never* try a new dish on guests unless you have tested it first. That's a tough rule for John. Always has to be cute. I blame it on our mother letting him play with Barbie dolls as a kid, but he says he just likes to be elegant. Yeah, OK, sure.

John: "I'll let you be in my dream, if you let me be in yours". I think Bob Dylan said that. And I categorically deny playing with Barbie dolls. They were way after my childhood. All I had were sock monkeys!

Our Heritage (a heart-warming story)

The Italian Peasant: Giovanni Napoleone

John: We called him "Grampa". He was our mother's father. Our mother called him "Dad", and our father respectfully called him "John". By himself when he was sixteen, he left the little mountain town of Ateleta in the Abruzzi, a region in the mountains east of Rome, in steerage of a steamship. I remember being told that he worked as a water boy on the railroad as a kid. But he later became a barber in the Italian neighborhood of Niagara Falls, New York. It was a fairly respected profession among Italians. He met his wife Maria Rosso who was the daughter of immigrants from Calabria. They had four daughters, beautiful auburn-haired girls who at school, with the last name of Napoleon, claimed they were French so they wouldn't be tagged "wops".

Grampa and Gramma Napoleone

Patrick: There is something to be said for the food that was eaten, in our mother's youth, and for the general level of physical activity back then. People *did* live to ripe old ages when all was said and done. The census bureau may say that people are living longer today, but they fail to mention that it is most likely because of advanced drugs and expensive medical techniques. But that aside, the additional years gained these days are years of being technically alive, not actually *living*.

John: Grampa lived a full, *living* life until he died in his late eighties. He usually made spaghetti and meatballs when he came to visit, and he always served one small portion to each of us at a time, so that no one would waste anything. He told me that in his youth he only had a piece of bread a day as he worked in the fields. He said he'd never wanted to return to Italy, with a disgusted curl in his lip and a sneer in his voice. He typically wore a starched shirt and a tie, and wore arm garters to keeps his shirt cuffs pulled up and clean. He always retained a strong Italian accent which made him very hard to understand. In the Italian neighborhood where he lived his whole life, an Italian dialect was the everyday language.

Patrick: He was the cook in the family, besides having music as his sanctuary and barbering as his profession. Our Gramma Mary ruled the roost and was very strict, from what our mother says. She was the overseer of the home and made sure the daughters were raised properly. Together, Giovanni and Maria made the perfect Italian couple.

John: I visited Ateleta, Grandpa's birthplace in Abruzzi when I was about forty years old. It was destroyed by retreating German forces during World War II, but largely re-built by public funds afterwards. It is spectacularly beautiful country, but poor. There is a tradition of young men leaving home to earn money to send back to their families, so they could survive, or leave too. There is a tradition in the Abruzzi of celebrating the return of a son from say Germany or America, by holding a huge feast – an extravaganza that belies the scarcity of food. It is almost unbelievably described by Waverley Root in his written "documentary", The Food of Italy.

> ⊗ *"… there are at least 30 courses, and they have been known to run to 60 … three fish dishes, mountain ham, country bread and mountain butter; double consommé; boiled meats … mortadella, guitar macaroni, fritters in celery sauce, grilled trout, roast kid, potato omelet, and artichokes fried with cheese … sausages, cardoon soup, veal rolls with beans, eel country style and grilled mutton with salad rich in mountain herbs … braised artichoke hearts, broccoli in sauce, galantine of chicken in jelly, pickles and artichokes in olive oil, deep fried brains and utility meats, veal with tuna sauce and capers, chicken hunter's style, and lamb chops … sweet-and-crazy pig's liver, kidneys, rock partridge with ham, veal scaloppini with truffles, and peas with ham … roasted scamorza ham, pecorino cheese, dried and fresh fruits, cookies and noci attorate … the meal was washed down with local wines".* And degistivi, I suspect.

When I visited Ateleta the only local restauranteur sat us down and brought a huge bowl of pasta to start. We started to serve ourselves portions from the bowl, but soon other bowls of the same pasta were brought, one for each of us. This was followed by a gigantic platter of fried lamb chops. Our palates were cleansed with a salad, the size of which probably depleted someone's local garden. As I entered the town, I had remembered seeing the older widowed women, dressed in black, combing the local fields for wild early dandelion greens and salad herbs. That was lunch. Still stuffed after sundown we hung out at the local bar drinking coffee and degistivi, watching the old men play cards into the wee hours.

There was only one other car in town when I was there. It belonged to a young man who had left to work in Germany. My closest relative in Ateleta was a very old cousin, several times removed, who showed me the town's cemetery, and who shared sausage, preserved in pork fat, and brandy with me at ten o'clock in the morning. I found my grandfather's birth certificate at the municipio building with the help of a friendly administrator who toasted the early morning occasion with more sweet wine. I visited the street where my grandfather was born, *Via Napoleone*. The town was a military garrison of Napoleon Bonaparte when he was King of Naples. Napoleon had red hair, I think. I met a young read-haired school girl in Ateleta who looked like Hilary, my daughter. I imagine that my ancestry is partially French, from a young French soldier who once convinced a poor, pretty girl that he was Bonaparte himself.

Patrick: Johnny sticks to this red hair theory of his as if he witnessed the whole thing. Although there *may* be some truth to it, I wholly doubt that armies were responsible for fair hair Italians which occur throughout Italy. Border relationships no doubt took place and spawned some mixed traits for different countries.

John: Alas, I am the romantic in the family. Patrick is the nit-picker, the "historian". Still, for all that heritage, as kids we rarely ate Italian food at home, because my father was prejudiced, being that his ancestors had been on one of the "original" boats from Europe, along with "The Mayflower Madame", Sidney Biddle Barrows. A family myth no doubt. I only remember the spaghetti and meatballs that Grampa made when he visited, the pizza my sister made when my father was away on business, and the ravioli my mother's cousin made on visits. I can still picture this very large man, in his sleeveless undershirt, rolling a massive sheet of pasta on our kitchen table, sweating copiously into it constantly, and making ravioli stuffed with ricotta and fresh spinach from our garden, and sauce, very light and brothy, of fresh tomatoes, also from our garden.

Patrick: Our mother was an average cook who prepared, for the most part, what our father wanted. Italian food was not on the list. Besides, our mother never learned how to cook, really, until she got married. This was a total waste and loss of valuable information from her father, gone forever. However, she cooked simply, using available ingredients, which again is a theme of this book. This mainly came from growing up in the depression and learning to be *extremely* frugal with everything, not just food.

John: And Pat rags on me for being frugal! Sheesh! But I often think of the things my mother told me she ate as a kid, such as escarole with white beans, pasta in broth, and the most exciting of all, a large pot of steaming polenta, on Sundays only, poured onto the bare wood of the kitchen table where it oozed to the perimeter. This was topped with a pot of tomato sauce and sausage. The family gathered around the table each with a fork, and ate their way to the middle of the table. The table, you see, gave up its amalgamation of flavors from the week's recipes being chopped and prepared on its surface, to the fresh polenta. To this day I can't imagine any meal being any more spectacular or more honest.

The English Peasant: Uncle Claude

John: Uncle Claude Barrows was our grandfather's brother. Claude became our father's surrogate father when his own dad died. Claude was a farmer near Lockwood, New York. He had some dairy cows, some pigs, and chickens. He and his wife, Rose, were self-sufficient, only generating cash from selling cream, eggs, and other such produce. They only purchased such staples as sugar, salt, or Red Man chewing tobacco. Everything from butter to soap was home made. The farm was poor and the land very sloped, rocky and timbered. Claude milled all his own hardwood, usually cherry and maple, and he made fine furniture with it. Our father took some of the aged cherry wood after Claude died and had a table made from it, which Patrick now has. It is a replica of a table, made by Claude's father, John, my great-grandfather, who lived nearby Claude. Hilary has the original kitchen table. And one day will give it to Dylan, her son, or Lily, her daughter. When we were kids, our family visited Uncle Claude and Aunt Rose in the summers, and during deer hunting season in the Fall. There was no plumbing in Claude's house. The outhouse was across the dirt road which separated the house from the barn and a creek that ran behind the barn. A hand pump in the kitchen pumped water from a spring outside. Water was heated in a reservoir in the kitchen's wood stove.

Uncle Claude Barrows

Aunt Rose Barrows

Patrick: Don't ever take your warm indoor toilet for granted! On those cold mornings one often walked through frigid air to that outhouse with good intentions, only to walk away un-fulfilled due to the shear cold when one's body kind of said, "closed for business until warmer weather or at least until somebody else warms up the seat first".

John: In the mornings Claude and Rose got up early to milk the cows by hand, and crank the separator which produced cream and skim milk. Rose baked bread in the wood oven, and always cooked oatmeal, bacon, eggs, and pancakes for breakfast. Claude and Rose, already "retired" when I first knew them, kept a huge garden. Beans, beets, carrots, tomatoes and so forth were canned. Potatoes, turnips, onions, apples, and winter squash were stored in the earthen cellar beneath the house. A cow was butchered before Winter, and its meat too was canned. Every year my father bought two piglets for Claude to raise. In the Fall, the pigs, grown and fattened on kitchen scraps and some grain, were killed, scalded and scraped, and hung and butchered. The head was boiled for headcheese, the hocks and hams smoked, and the intestines used to encase the ground pork meat preserving the rest of the pig as sausage. I would watch the slaughtering and butchering from atop the fence. Thus I learned where meat came from.

What We Ate

John: Our father also kept a big garden. He and our mother canned or froze everything. My brothers and I were made to harvest all of the crops of the wild berries that grew around our house – strawberry's the size of buckshot, elderberries, gooseberries, blueberries, red (and yellow and purple) raspberries, currants, and wild grapes. All for jellies and jams. Our father made pickles obsessively. Mustard pickles, bread-and-butter pickles, one-a-day pickles, and pickles for which I've forgotten the names. And he made chili sauce by simmering the summer's tomatoes all day in spices until it became a dark red pungent, sweet "catsup", which is all we ever ate on our meatloaf and baked ham. He was the "foodie" in the family. Not necessarily the best cook, but the most obsessive.

Patrick: He pushed his kids. He had us doing all kinds of labor whether it was necessary or not. Like, "you need to pick up twigs in the lawn". He always found something for us to do. Especially if had something to do with harvesting food, weeding the garden, or hulling tiny wild strawberries, and so forth.

John: Also like our having to help Mom wash all the dishes after each meal. There were always six of us at dinner. Mom and Dad ("Ma" and "Pa" as they called each other) and the three boys and one girl. Dinner was always something like chicken and dumplings, or pot roast, or meatloaf, or escalloped potatoes with pork sausage, or liver and onions with bacon, or "slumgullion" (our father's version of goulash), or cheese soufflé, or pork chops and applesauce, or baked ham and sweet potatoes. Diverging from this traditional fare occasionally my mother made shrimp Creole, a recipe from their WWII days in Mobile when shrimp was the most affordable protein. Or my father would re-create his favorite dishes from his favorite restaurants in the cities he traveled to on business, such as "pepper steak" or "shrimp scampi Madrid", as he called it. In the summer we ate lots of fresh water perch and bass we caught from Lake Ontario, the fillets only dipped in cornmeal and fried in salt pork fat, and fresh green beans stewed in whole milk and butter with lots of pepper. But my favorite food of all was the cans of frozen Campbell's snapping turtle soup he brought back from Philadelphia. A thick soup so rich and brown and redolent of sherry and brandy that even as a kid I knew I had discovered something extraordinary.

Patrick: Campbell's eventually stopped producing that soup, which by the way was only found in the frozen food section. Bookbinders, a restaurant in Philly, put out their rendition, unfrozen, but it never stacked up.

John: Pat never told me that Campbell's stopped making that soup! Come to think of it, he probably was the one that told me Santa Claus wasn't real. The lessons I learned from all this have remained with me, thankfully to this day. We eat simple things that taste good, and always will taste good regardless of the newest "fusion" statements in food. We didn't eat ourselves to death. One chicken fed six people, or a Sunday pot roast fed all six of us with enough left over for hash on Monday. We didn't eat prepared foods, with a special dispensation for the above-mentioned snapping turtle soup. We ate fresh or home-canned foods. My father resorted to buying live chickens from local farmers and cut off their heads himself, to my younger brothers' chagrin, because he couldn't stand eating frozen chicken from the local super markets. And he would only eat corn if he could get it from the farmer and cook it within an hour after it was picked. And last, but not at all least, as kids we simply didn't eat if we didn't like what was cooked. There was no discussion. There was no debate. It was not a child-based democracy.

Patrick: Oh come on! He only did the live chicken thing once. I was with him when he went to the farm and bought two chickens and put them in a burlap bag. It was winter. We arrived home, he got out the axe and a chopping block. If you ever heard the saying. "running around like a chicken with its head cut off", that's exactly what happened, and I took off running the other way thoroughly convinced that these headless monsters were chasing me!

John: It was in the summer, not the winter. Ah, thankfully my mind isn't going as fast as Patrick's. But he has an excuse. He was fairly young at that point. As I remember it, the "monster" really did chase him down the gravel driveway as he ran a mile a minute in his bare feet, while the headless chicken seemingly tried to land on his head

Recipes That We Ate Growing Up

John: This is our childhood food history. It's not here as part of our so-called instruction on how to cook using a "Tuscan-Provençal-Peasant" model. But you may find it entertaining, or you may even think the recipes are worth trying out. However what you may discover while perusing it is that you begin to remember your own family food history. And how you may choose to bring that history forward into your current life, and into your kids', and their kids', lives.

"Slumgullion"

Patrick: This is a rare case where I have used a prepared concoction like canned tomato soup. I could try a variation and use tomatoes for example, but I want to keep this as original as can be if for no other reason, it was one of my father's cooking successes, and if it ain't broke, don't fix it!

Our father was not a great cook, however that did not stop him from tinkering in the kitchen once in a while. Thankfully his "Duck a l'Orange" never made it past his first attempt when he just took a can of thawed frozen orange juice and poured on top of the duck that was in the oven. There was a lot left over, including birdshot, on that one! Slumgullion, as he named it, was a recipe he excelled at. Where it came from I do not know. I always tended to think it was printed on the side of a tomato soup can since it does call for tomato soup. Either way, he done good. I remember this oldie from at least 40 years ago and I have only made slight modifications to the ingredients and process. Believe me, this is an excellent dish, especially during the cold months. To this day I make it at least every other month, by request!

INGREDIENTS: Ground beef, a little olive oil, sweet Italian sausage in casing, chopped onion and garlic, condensed tomato soup, dry basil, dry oregano, ground fennel seed (if the sausage contains no fennel), tomato paste, cooked elbow macaroni.

- Add the oil to the pot.
- Add the onions and sauté.
- Add the beef, and brown.
- Add the garlic, basil, oregano, fennel.
- Add the soup and water.
- Bring to a simmer.
- Add the sausages, and simmer for a few hours or so with the top on, stirring occasionally.
- Add the tomato paste.
- Let simmer with the top ajar so the Slumgullion reduces slightly.
- When it is thick and rich, but not dried out, it is done. Stir in the cooked macaroni and serve.

Swiss Steak

Patrick: Don't ask me where the name came from or if there is a standard "Swiss Steak" out there somewhere. I don't know, I really don't care, and it doesn't matter. This is Ma's recipe. It's simple and it also calls for the infamous Campbells tomato soup. Nevertheless, a great example of what we ate growing up.

INGREDIENTS: Top or bottom round steak, flour, onion, condensed tomato soup.

You want a cheap piece of meat but it should be lean. It will braise for awhile and *eventually* become tender.

- Sprinkle the meat on both sides with flour and then pound between 2 sheets of waxed paper. The meat should be thin and then cut into serving-sized pieces. If the cut is thick then you will have slice it into 2 thinner pieces before pounding.
- Heat some oil in a pan and sauté some onion in it.
- Add the meat, the can of tomato soup and a little water.
- Slowly cook this for a few hours until the meat is tender. You may want to add water a little at a time if it's too thick.
- Add salt and pepper to taste.

This was usually served with mashed potatoes, a vegetable of some kind or maybe Ma's cheese "soufflé" that was made with cornflakes of all things and wasn't really a soufflé.

John: Actually, "Ma", our mother, could never resist tinkering with recipes, though mostly she would do this to simplify things or cut back on preparation time.

Shrimp Creole

Patrick: This is a recipe that no doubt Ma and Pa picked up while doing their short stint down south in Mobile during WWII. Again, I never tinkered with it. It is what it is and that's good enough.

INGREDIENTS: Oil, flour, onion, garlic, green pepper, parsley, Worcestershire sauce, chili pepper flakes, bay leaf, celery seed, thyme.

- Make a roux with some oil and flour.
- Let this cook a little, stirring until brown.
- Add the chopped onions, garlic, green pepper, parsley.
- Sauté until onion begins to brown slightly.
- Add canned chopped tomatoes, Worcestershire sauce, red pepper flakes, salt, bay leaves, celery seed and thyme.

Sometimes, if she had it, she would use a bottled concoction called "gumbo file", the ground root or leaf of a sassafras tree. Let this all simmer slowly until it thickens. A few minutes before serving, add cleaned raw shrimp to the mixture. Served over rice.

"Shrimp Scampi Madrid"

John: Another little something I think our Dad picked up in a restaurant somewhere. I think he made up the name though, as I kinda think using both the words "shrimp" and "scampi" is a little redundant.

INGREDIENTS: The largest un-shelled and freshest shrimp you can find, butter, garlic, salt, pepper, and maybe a little dry white vermouth though I'm not sure if my father used any kind of de-glazing liquid.

- Shell, de-vein, and butterfly the shrimp, leaving them whole.
- Chop lots of garlic.
- Melt lots of butter in a sauté pan.
- Add the garlic and sauté lightly.
- Add the shrimp and barely cook through, but browning lightly, stirring with a wooden spoon.
- Spoon the shrimp onto a serving dish.
- Deglaze the pan with vermouth and pour over the shrimp.
- Sprinkle some chopped parsley over the dish.

This was eaten very hot as an appetizer or early separate course.

Pepper Steak

John: Another one of our Dad's specialties. Another restaurant steal, no doubt. He wasn't creative, but he was obsessive about a few dishes, and he liked good basic food.

INGREDIENTS: A good cut of beef, like a "London broil", top round, New York strip etc. (or as expensive a boneless cut as you want), black peppercorns, sherry.

- Grind the peppercorns very coarsely, or put them in a cotton towel and crush them with a mallet or rolling pin on a wood work surface.
- Pound a good layer of crushed pepper into each side of the steak with a mallet.
- Put a pat of butter on top of the steak and broil in a heavy broiling pan under a very hot oven broiler.
- Turn over, add another pat of butter, and broil the other side.
- Keep it rare.
- Remove broiling pan to a medium hot stove-top burner.
- Put steak on a platter and salt it.
- Add some sherry to the hot pan, stirring and de-glazing.
- Slice the steak across the grain into quarter inch slices.
- Pour the sauce over the sliced steak.

Served with a German potato salad which I think he got it from a can. We'd always soak up the "jus" with lots of fresh Italian bread.

Sauer Braten and Potato Pancakes

John: When I was about twelve, we lived in the country on a main north-south highway in upstate New York, before there was a major four lane freeway linking southern New York and Canada. On this highway, near our house, was a seasonal summer hamburger stand called "The Gopher Hole". It was operated by a hefty German immigrant woman who I think was a war bride. She had a son, my age, who "helped" her out at the stand. He and I got to be good summertime friends, and mainly we ate hamburgers, French fries, and hot dogs all day. My father, as I've explained, loved to search out new recipes, and convinced her to share her recipes for sauer braten, sweet and sour red cabbage, and potato pancakes. A heavier concoction I've never eaten in my life. But oh so good!

INGREDIENTS FOR THE SAUER BRATEN: a large chuck roast, red wine vinegar, water, chopped onion, bay leaves, salt, peppercorns, sugar, fat for browning.

- Put the un-cooked roast into a deep non-reactive bowl or crock.
- Combine equal amounts of water and vinegar so that there is enough to cover the roast in the bowl, and add the other ingredients.
- Bring marinade to a boil and let cool.
- Pour over the roast in the bowl, and cover bowl with plastic wrap.
- Refrigerate for several days, making sure meat stays submerged, or turning it daily to expose all sides to the marinade.
- Remove meat from bowl and save marinade.
- Dry the roast very thoroughly with towels.
- Heat fat in Dutch oven and brown roast well on all sides.
- Add marinade back in and bring to a simmer on the stove.
- Cover the pot tightly and place in low-medium oven for several hours.
- Turn meat periodically to keep all sides exposed to liquid.
- When done, remove meat and let rest on a serving platter.
- Thicken cooking liquid, if necessary, with a flour and water mixture.

Serve sliced with gravy, potato pancakes, and braised sweet-and-sour red cabbage.

INGREDIENTS FOR POTATO PANCAKES: Coarsely grated raw peeled potatoes, eggs, flour, baking powder, milk, salt, pepper, some grated onion.

- Grate the potatoes and onion into a bowl of cold water and let soak for a few minutes.
- Drain well and dry well in cotton towels.
- Add enough beaten egg, flour, milk, a little baking powder, salt and pepper to make a fairly stiff batter, but one you can still spoon into hot fat and will spread out like a pancake.
- In a large heavy skillet heat the fat.
- Drop large spoonfuls of the batter into the hot fat, few at a time in batches.
- Brown well on both sides.
- Drain finished pancakes on paper towels on a serving dish in a warm oven, while you finish all the batches.

It was *not* advisable to eat too much of this Teutonic threesome at any one sitting. While the taste was exquisite, the impact on the digestive system was prolonged.

Chicken and Dumplings

Patrick: (I keep telling Johnny that I don't have a freaking chicken and dumplings recipe, so you'll have to find your own. But it was something we ate a lot. It was basically a chicken stewed with vegetables, thickened when done, and then covered with handfuls of sticky dumpling dough which cooked under a heavy lid).

Escalloped Potatoes

Patrick: (I don't have this damn recipe either, though I'm sure John fondly remembers eating this. Alas, our mother is now largely mentally deficient in the memory department, and asking her to dictate it to me would be an exercise in futility. It was creamy and thick and as Johnny remembers often included slices of leftover baked ham or handmade pork sausage patties).

Meat Loaf with Chili Sauce

Patrick: I use ground chuck for this. Chili sauce recipe is fabulous, but it's a family secret and we would not divulge it to anyone!

INGREDIENTS: Ground chuck, an egg, unseasoned bread crumbs, chili sauce, some chopped parsley and onion, thyme, salt & pepper.

- Mix everything together very well in a bowl with your hands. It should be moist.
- Put into a Pyrex loaf pan.
- Do not pack down too firmly.
- Spread some additional chili sauce on top.
- Put some uncooked bacon slices on top.
- Put into preheated moderate oven until it's cooked through and the bacon is crisped.
- Remove, pour off grease, remove to serving plate, and slice.

Served with more chili sauce.

"Cagoots"

John: Well, that's how it sounds, though I have no idea what it means or how to spell the actual name, if there is one. It may be some Italian dialectical name for some sort of zucchini type squash. Here's my mother's recipe.

INGREDIENTS: Onion, potatoes, zucchini, tomatoes, hot chili pepper flakes, parsley.

- Sauté some onion in olive oil in a soup pot.
- Add some cubed potatoes and sauté until slightly brown.
- Add zucchini cut up into chunks, and stir while browning lightly.
- Add some fresh chopped tomatoes.
- Add a chopped hot chili.
- Simmer until done, but not too mushy. Though the consistency should thicken a little and the vegetables should meld together a little. More stew-like than soupy.

Our mother only added parsley. Eaten while dunking in chunks of fresh Italian bread.

Patrick: OK, "the master" screwed up the cagoots! He is soooo out of touch, it isn't funny!

Cagoots, cagootza, etc. is a very common Italian peasant dish with slight variations. I guess his, above, is a variation of the senior moment variety.

Here is how to *really* make Cagoots:
- Put some olive oil in an enameled pot.
- Heat and add diced potato and a sliced onion.
- Sauté until a little browned.
- Add peeled and cubed zucchini and a little water and let steam a few minutes, covered. Add a can of chopped tomatoes, not pureed, not crushed, not whole, but *chopped!*
- Add dried basil, oregano, salt, and pepper.
- Reduce heat and simmer with cover ajar and let reduce some.
- Should take about an hour.

There you have it folks!

Calf Liver (yuck) with Bacon and Onions

INGREDIENTS: Calf (not cow or steer) liver, bacon, onions, flour.

- Render bacon until crisp, and remove to dish, leaving all the bacon fat in the pan
- Fry onions in fat until well caramelized, and remove to plate with bacon.
- Lightly dredge the liver in flour, and sauté it in the fat. Put on the plate with bacon and onions.

Served with mashed potatoes that were covered with melted butter, salt and pepper, and finely chopped onion.

Campbell's Snapping Turtle Soup

INGREDIENTS: A can of Campbell's frozen snapping turtle soup.

- Put the frozen soup into a saucepan, and add a can of water.
- Over medium heat, slowly stir until the frozen concentrate is melted and the soup is thick and hot.

If you can find this soup, please let us know where! I've given up asking Santa for some.

Fried Fish with Salt Pork

John: This is made only in the summer, on weekends, with fresh yellow lake perch and largemouth black bass fillets, from Henderson or Sackets Harbors, on Lake Ontario.

INGREDIENTS: Skinless and boneless fillets, cornmeal, salt pork, pepper.

- Fry strips of salt pork in a heavy cast iron skillet until crispy and well rendered of fat.
- Eat the fried salt pork as an appetizer while the fish is cooking
- Dredge the fillets in cornmeal and fry until crispy in the salt pork fat.

Eaten hot with Italian bread. Our mother always made us eat bread with fish, just in case we choked on a stray bone. The bread theoretically would dislodge the bone.

John: Historical Note on Fish.
Cleaning and filleting fish was my job, being the oldest of three boys. When we returned from fishing, our father would go into the house, pour a highball, and start frying up the salt pork. I was left in the middle of the vegetable garden, with my weekly horrible sunburn (while the mosquitoes made it worse) to clean and fillet several dozen fish. I soon developed a fast system out of necessity.

- Using a very sharp small blade of a pocket knife, make 2 shallow slits along each side of the fish's back from head to tale.
- On both sides of the fish make a cut from the head end of the first slit all the way down to the bottom of the fish.
- Then make a slit starting at the bottom of the above slit all the way along the bottom of the fish to the tale.
- With a very sharp fillet knife, carefully separate the fillets from the fish running the knife along the backbone slits and following the bone structure of the fish with the knife's tip, until the fillet is completely detached.
- With the fillet on the cleaning plank, skin side down, run the knife carefully between the skin and the flesh starting at the tail end of the fillet, until the skin is removed in one piece. What's left is an intact fish, head and all, without its fillets. Throw this into a freshly dug hole in the garden as fertilizer, or for enterprising raccoons.

Green Beans in Milk and Butter

John: This was good with yellow wax beans or green beans.

INGREDIENTS: Fresh green or yellow bush or pole beans, milk, butter, salt, pepper

- Cut the beans into say one inch lengths
- Blanch and cool them quickly in cold water and drain
- Put into a saucepan and add some whole milk, and or cream
- Finish cooking until still slightly crunchy.
- Add some butter and salt and pepper.

This will be eaten in small bowls with the beans swimming in a pool of buttery milk.

Bean (or Meatloaf) Sandwiches

These are great with Molson or Labatt's Canadian beer, taken on fishing trips on Lake Ontario to catch those perch and bass for fish fries on summer weekends.

INGREDIENTS: Leftover cold baked beans and/or meatloaf, sliced white bread, mustard.

- Spread leftover baked beans, or slabs of cold leftover meatloaf, on slices of basic store-bought, packaged white bread.
- Slather on French's yellow mustard.
- Wrap in wax paper.
- Place in the ice chest with the beer.

Eaten as soon as you were hungry, or bored, on the boat. Our Dad let us have a sip of beer. But we drank "pop".

Potato Salad

INGREDIENTS: Boiling potatoes, white wine vinegar, yellow prepared mustard, spicy prepared mustard, sugar, mayonnaise, radishes, scallions, hard-boiled eggs.

- Boil potatoes whole, in their skins.
- Drain and cool in a bowl in the refrigerator
- When cool, peel them and cut into small cubes.
- Hard boil and cool some eggs
- Make a dressing of white wine vinegar, salt, pepper, sugar, Dijon or a spicy mustard, French's mustard, mayonnaise.
- Chop some radishes and scallions and add to the potatoes
- Peel and slice the eggs and add
- Pour over the dressing and mix

Filled Cookies

Patrick: This was Johnny's favorite, as I hate raisins, and Ma *always* made them for *him*. As with all baking, recipe amounts are more specific than what we usually give.

Cookie Pastry:
INGREDIENTS: 2 eggs, 2 C sugar, 1C shortening (solid Crisco), 1 C milk, 2 tsp baking soda, 1 tsp salt, 6 C flour, 2 tsp baking powder. 1 tsp vanilla

- Cut shortening into flour then add the other ingredients to form a dough. Roll out to about 1/8 thick. Cut dough into approx 3" circles.

Filling:
INGREDIENTS: 2 C raisins, 1 C sugar, 1 1/2 C cold water, 2 tbsp white vinegar

- Combine ingredients, cook until thick, and let cool.

Assemble:
- Put a heaping dollop of filling onto each round cutout and place another round cutout on top and seal the edge by using a little water and pressing together.
- Bake on greased and floured baking sheet at 350 until lightly golden.

Cinnamon Twists

Patrick: This was one of *my* favorites and Ma always made them for *me,* but everyone else usually grabbed them. These can be a chore to make but it is worth the effort. A nice calm atmosphere is best without hell breaking loose all over.

For The Yeast Dough:
INGREDIENTS: 1 C sour cream, 2 tbsp shortening, 3 tbsp sugar, 1/8 tsp baking soda, 1 tsp salt, 1 large unbeaten egg, 1 packet of dry yeast, 3 C flour

Filling:
INGREDIENTS: 2 tbsp softened butter, ½ C light brown sugar, 1 tsp cinnamon

Prepare The Dough:
- Bring the sour cream to boil in large sauce pan
- Remove from heat.
- Combine the oil, sugar, baking soda and salt, add to the sour cream and stir.
- Cool until lukewarm
- Add the egg and the yeast and stir until yeast is dissolved.
- Gradually add the flour with a spoon and mix together
- Turn out onto a lightly floured pastry board and knead a few times to form a smooth ball. Cover with waxed paper and let rest for about 5 minutes.
- Roll out dough into a rectangle about 6" x 24" by ¼" thick.

- Spread the entire surface with the softened butter.
- Combine the brown sugar and cinnamon and sprinkle the half the dough length wise.
- Now fold over the other side of the dough so now you have a rectangle about 3" x 24". Press edges and top to seal the filling in.
- Using a sharp knife cut 24 strips approx 1" wide.
- Taking each strip at both ends, twist in opposite directions forming a spiral stick.
- Place on a greased baking sheet about 2" apart pressing both ends of the sticks firmly and flatly to the cookie sheet.
- Cover with a cloth and let rise for about 2 hours.
- Bake in 375 degree oven for about 12-15 minutes.

Cooled before icing with a mixture of confectioner's sugar and milk.

Pot Roast

John: This is the American version of sauer braten, without all the marinating.

INGREDIENTS: Pot roast, carrots, onions, potatoes, oil, flour.

- Put some oil in a Dutch oven and brown the roast well on all sides.
- Remove the roast and brown the onions, carrots, and potatoes lightly.
- Add back the roast, and add water to almost cover.
- Put the top on and cook slowly until the roast is tender.
- Thicken the liquid with a flour/water paste. Or you could add a little tomato paste during cooking as a thickening agent. It also adds another flavor.
- Salt and pepper to taste.

Beef Hash

INGREDIENTS: Leftover pot roast, potatoes, onion, and carrots from Sunday's pot roast.

- Grind or chop finely everything up and mix will together.
- Fry the mixture in butter until it has a slight browned crust.
- Serve individual helping with a large cooking spoon.
- Pour ketchup or chili sauce on each helping.

Pork Chops and Applesauce With Mashed Potatoes

John: This is dedicated to our brother, Bobby, who was between Patrick and me in age. He died as a very young adult in an industrial accident in West Virginia. This was his favorite meal – though not by a large margin, since he was the only overweight (but only slightly) person in the family.

INGREDIENTS: Bone-in pork chops, potatoes boiled and mashed with butter and milk, applesauce from a jar, butter, onion.

- Fry the pork chops with salt and pepper until done.
- Chop onion finely.

Served with a helping of potatoes with melted butter, chopped onion, salt and pepper. Booby would have advised to use a napkin to pick up the pork chop with one's fingers, and gnaw it to the bone, dipping each bite into the apple sauce.

Iceberg Lettuce Salad

INGREDIENTS: A head of iceberg lettuce, salt, pepper, vegetable oil, vinegar.

- Wash the head of lettuce, and peel off the outer wilted leafs
- Cut the head into quarters.
- Serve each person a lettuce quarter drizzled with a vinaigrette of salt, pepper, oil, and vinegar.

Sloppy Joes

Patrick: One of my first early dishes I could make. Probably dates back 35 years. I still make it today maybe four times a year. And I still enjoy it.

INGREDIENTS: Lean ground beef, onion chopped, celery stalk chopped, ketchup, lemon juice, dry mustard, Worcestershire sauce, brown sugar, dash of cumin, salt & pepper, some olive oil.

- Sauté the onion and celery in some olive oil.
- Add the beef and cook until crumbled and done.
- Add the ketchup, lemon juice, dry mustard, Worcester sauce, brown sugar, cumin and mix all together.
- Let this mixture simmer and reduce until fairly thick.
- You may need to add more ketchup if it doesn't seem "tomatoey" enough.
- Salt and pepper to taste.

Served on hamburger buns with cole slaw.

John: We also would, not infrequently, just have pancakes and fried eggs for supper. No need to add the recipe for that here. But when I think about it, it was an awfully wonderful supper, and even a little decadent. Like eating breakfast at night.

How We Learned To Cook

"When you can appreciate the virtues of a salad of crisp green beans, seasoned with nothing more than salt, olive oil, and lemon juice, you have understood Italian eating at its best – simple, direct, and inexhaustibly good." Marcella Hazan, The Classic Italian Cookbook.

John: As I write this, Thanksgiving is approaching, and recipes for the holiday meal start popping up in the local newspaper. I am fortunate to live in Oregon, where there is a rapidly growing food culture that demands fresh, local, organic meat, wild fish, and vegetables. And a burgeoning restaurant scene that is getting raves nationally. Yet this morning I noted three recipes in our local rag, by three chefs of three of the most noted local restaurants. Keeping in mind Ms. Hazan's quote above, here are what these three young chefs suggested as "new twists" on classic side dishes. One suggested cipollini onions (an earthy, sweet, and expensive treat) covered with a caramel made of *2* cups of sugar and *2* cups of sherry vinegar (and other strongly flavored ingredients). Another chef recommended sweet potatoes covered with a sauce of a whole stick of butter, a cup of bourbon, a cup of brown sugar (among other additions). The third took those same fresh green beans that Marcella adored, and ladled upon them a sauce of (for just pound of beans) *7* tablespoons of butter, *2* cups of whole milk, plus a cup of flour and a cup of breadcrumbs. She also wasted a pound of expensive wild chanterelles under this concoction. I am not arguing that the resultant dishes that these three created didn't taste good. But what they tasted of was bourbon, sugar, butter, milk, mushrooms, vinegar, and shallots – plus thyme, rosemary, onion, parsley, and garlic. *Not* sweet potatoes, beans, or cipollini. I'm not quite sure what their point was in making up these recipes. Maybe it's all in keeping with what people these days think good food is all about. But I know for a fact that it's not about the tradition of good food, in any culture.

Patrick: What a hoot! It is stories like that that make this book so important. It is most typical to find the bastardizing of simple food in the more upscale restaurants and most noticeably by younger chefs. This is all fine and well if you enjoy "fusionistic" food styling when dining out, but this book is about dining in and what you create, with the time you have and your desire to do it. Ok, proceed, bro'.

John: Be that as it may, there was a lengthy hiatus between the well-fed years of my childhood and the day I really began to take a real interest in cooking good food. There were those years in college where I was lucky enough to have a fraternity brother whose father owned Rolling Rock Brewery. I considered beer nature's perfect food. Then the years of young parenthood in graduate school when the diet, whose food budget was $9.00 a week, consisted of a lot of beans and rice. Then I arrived in New York City, started working in the fashion industry, and began to travel extensively around the country and the world. Trips to Florence and Prato to buy fabric. Trips to Hong Kong to source production. And trips to Atlanta, Chicago, San Francisco, Houston, Los Angeles, Boston, and Seattle to meet with customers. I began to frequent my favorite restaurants in each city, and I began to appreciate the richness and diversity of America and the world.

One day I walked into a book store and bought **Mastering The Art of French Cooking,** by Julia Child, Louisette Bertholle, and Simone Beck (a book and people I'd heard of and seen on TV) and a book called **The Fine Art of Italian Cooking** by Giuliani Bugialli, a chef with a very long Florentine pedigree - someone I'd never heard of. At home I picked up Giuliano's book first, since it was about Italian food. As a Florentine, Giuliano propounded the almost unbelievable theory that all great European cuisines started in Tuscany, and that indeed the high art of Tuscan cuisine was hi-jacked by Catherine de Medici to France in the 16th century to the then un-shaven Gauls and Neanderthals of that part of the world. Hmmmm … an interesting proposition. So I started cooking from the Bugialli text. But within a few short weeks I stopped. This wasn't the Italian cooking I grew up with. There was barely any tomato sauce. There were no meatballs. Instead there were three inch thick steaks grilled over hot oak coals and served simply with a sprinkling of salt. The squid wasn't deep-fried, but stuffed with its own tentacles and braised in olive oil and white wine. Ravioli was stuffed with squash and nutmeg and drizzled with butter infused with fresh sage. Lasagna was made with nutmeg scented balsamella (i.e. béchamel) sauce and layered with fresh pasta made with spinach. This just wasn't right. This was *not* Italian food. So I turned to Julia and began to cook. "Boeuf a la Mode", beef oven-braised for hours in a rich bullion of onion, garlic, carrot, celery, thyme, bay, parsley, allspice, red wine, brandy, and olive oil – with veal knuckle, calf's feet, bacon rind, beef stock added for more richness - and served with carrots braised in butter and small onions braised in brown stock. "Coq au Vin", chicken browned and braised in red wine, onions, mushrooms, cognac, butter, garlic, tomato paste, and bacon. With "buttered peas if you wanted a green vegetable". "Tart tatin", an amazing apple "pie" made with a crust of flour, salt, butter and egg yolks, and a filling of apples sautéed in butter and sugar. And served with whipped cream. Now this was eating! And cooking!

But there was something about that Tuscan book that nagged at me, and I picked it up once more. It did in fact remind me of the simplicity of the Italian food I'd grown up with, and indeed the American food I'd grown up with. Simple, unadorned, and straight-forward. So I went straight, arbitrarily, to "Peposo", a stew simply of chunks of beef shank simmered slowly in red wine, garlic, some tomato, and a *tablespoon* of black pepper. I was hooked. And this was at least twenty years before I ever saw or heard the term "Tuscan cuisine" uttered on American shores or as a sub-title under a restaurant's moniker. My bother and I started to cook the foods of Tuscany. Making fresh pasta for lasagna and ravioli, bread salad with tomato and basil, porcini mushroom tarts, focaccia, chickpea pancakes, pureed bean soup, kale with lemon and garlic, spinach gnocchi with butter-cream sauce, basil risotto, spicy Livorno fish soup, bistecca alla Fiorentina, tuna with fresh rosemary, asparagus with parsley-caper sauce, timbales of pureed beans and broccolirab, "biscotti di Prato" dunked in "Vin Santo", and fresh olives sautéed in olive oil with salt. To name a few.

One day, by chance I learned that Giuliano spent his winters in New York and held cooking classes in his apartment. We signed up. For weeks we cooked under his watchful eye, using mezzalunas to chop vegetables, forks to mix fresh pasta, and gratellas to roast meat on the stovetop. He "tsk-tsked" when the vegetables weren't chopped enough, when the pasta was too tough from adding too much flour, and if the garlic simmered too long and in the hot oil. He eschewed Cuisinarts. And he allowed us to do all the cooking, while he coached. I started to seek out Tuscan cooking in American restaurants where I traveled on business. I began to discover them in NY at "Il Cantinori" (probably the best Italian or Tuscan restaurant in the U.S.), and in Houston, San Francisco, London, Los Angeles, and Seattle. When I told people that I cooked Tuscan food, I always had to explain what it was.

"Well", I'd say, "It's meat simply roasted, fresh egg pasta without a lot of tomato sauce, cannellini beans cooked in a flask all day with a piece of pancetta and some sage leaves, the thinnest crust pizzas with just some fresh sliced tomatoes, fresh basil leaves, and buffalo mozzarella, and hard almond biscuits dipped in sweet brandy for dessert."

> 🍽️ But this isn't after all a cookbook about Tuscan cooking. It's about simple food, cooked well. And it's about mastering a few basic concepts, (processes or techniques, if you will, so that you can learn to cook without a cookbook or a recipe under your nose. It'll be a little biased to Mediterranean fare, I admit, because I understand that best. And I won't tell you about my adventures in Asian cooking, which I can't get my western head around. But it's the idea of simplicity that I'm propounding. You can use it in whatever cuisine you like.

Patrick: Alas, my beginnings were not as illustrious, and bordered more on the "seedier" side of life. The year was 1975 or 1976, or something like that. I was 20 years old or so, and had just gotten my first real full time job and my own apartment in the suburbs of NYC. I started out at the bottom at the job, and the apartment had next to nothing for furniture. The refrigerator had the usual staples of milk, mayo, mustard and ketchup. When you're that young you are not thinking about cooking your own food. There was other more "important" stuff to do. Besides, prepared food could be had on the cheap just about anywhere I went, and it was good.

After about two years, give or take, I moved to Connecticut. A bit of culture shock occurred. The convenience of good, inexpensive "city" food disappeared. As far as I was concerned, this state didn't have any good places to eat! If I wanted it, I had to cook it.
Sure, I had some knowledge of basic cooking but I had to learn to make what I liked, not what others thought I might like. Yeah, I made recipes out of cookbooks and more often than not they all got changed to adapt to my taste or else I trashed them. I was a peasant - cooking and eating what was inexpensive and available. My abilities grew, and I was more at home in the kitchen once I knew what it was I was wanted to do - create good food. Then one day (it may have been for my birthday) Johnny enrolled me in one of Giuliano Bugialli's cooking semesters in lower Manhattan. Keep in mind, Johnny knew who this guy was, but I guess decided to send me as the guinea pig to see what he and his classes were all about instead of going himself. Johnny later joined me in future lessons with Mr. Bugialli and neither one of us ever regretted it. Giuliano is "of the earth" in my eyes. He is not pretentious, but he is exacting. Being patient and exuding a passion for what he did spilled over onto his students. Nobody looked at him as a celebrity but as one of the guys, because that is the way he related to everyone. Now I had learned some new techniques and began to develop a real foundation on which to expand. I was ready to finally teach Johnny how to cook!

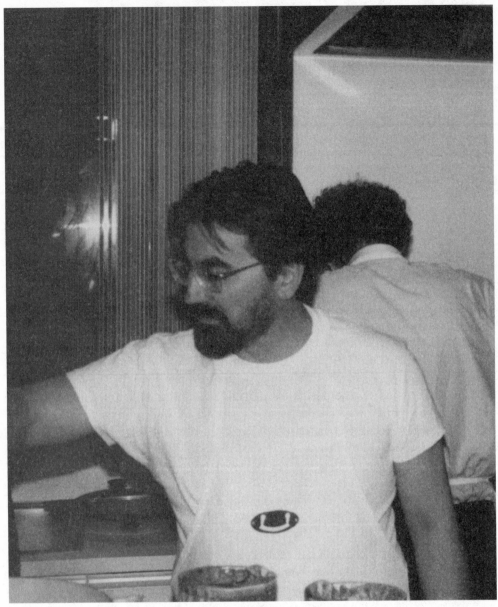
Giuliano

John: I have to admit to a senior moment here, because I don't remember that Patrick started taking classes with Giuliano before I did. Not that it matters. I've discarded a lot of data, primarily un-printable data, about what Patrick was up to in those days. I'll only tell you that after not having seen him for several years (he is 7 years my junior, and I was off to college, graduate school, and a career in NYC while he was driving our parents nuts in upstate New York) when one day as I was leaving the house in Larchmont to catch the train to Manhattan, he came bouncing down the street, smoking a joint, with all his worldly belongings in tow. A small back pack, a soccer ball, and bongo drums. He stayed with us for a while until my ex-wife "encouraged" him to move out and get a job . So now that the record is clarified, we can proceed.

Patrick: I never thanked Johnny for taking in the family street urchin, but he has to admit we had some fun, like playing "kitchen soccer", making sandwiches with 4" of peanut butter that you were not allowed *not* to eat, and the trips to Baskin Robbins for the ice cream fixes. Actually, his ex-wife told him to tell me to leave so they could carry on with their marital bliss. Turns out I did move out and Johnny followed suit years later. Guess who took *him* in? You got it!

John: Before I proceed one step further in this tome, I want to note Erick and Madeleine Vedel's influence. They introduced me to the nuances of traditional Provençal cuisine in their school, "Cuisine et Tradition School of Provençale Cuisine", in Arles. The cuisine of this region is much under-represented in the cooking literature here in the States, and rivals (in my opinion) Tuscan cuisine for its clean, subtle, and fresh simplicity.

Erick Vedel and John

Basic Flavors, Ingredients, Etc.

"Odori"

John: I may be technically mis-using this Italian term, but essentially it refers to herbs, spices, and other vegetables you might use to flavor and enhance your main recipe ingredients.

Patrick: Essentially, the term means "aromas", or in cooking, the aromatic herbs and/or vegetables at the base of what you are preparing.

John: I think that's what I said. Now he's starting to sound like my wife.

> 🍽 *The most basic ensemble of odori ingredients for soups, sauces, stews, braised meats, and so forth is a finely chopped mixture of Italian parsley, garlic, carrot, onion, and celery.*

Forget the time consuming process of chopping all the ingredients separately, then sweating the onions first, and then adding the others one by one. Just go ahead and chop the whole mess up together and dump it into some warmed olive oil in your pan and sauté just until it looks cooked and takes on a little color and smells good.

> 🍽 *As with all cooking, it's not about precise measurements and timing. As Chef Pino Luongo, the author of **A Tuscan in the Kitchen**, and the founder of the above-mentioned "Il Cantinori", would say in a typical recipe, "Enjoy the beautiful, strong smell of the sauce and vegetables. Your nose tells you 'This is good; let's keep it like this.' "*

Patrick: I have to question garlic in John's basic odori , and besides my voice is much lower than his wife's. I believe the basics are celery, carrot and onion and that's it. But I do agree, to chop as necessary to fit what you are preparing and throw it all into the pot. If you do add garlic, add it later so as not to overcook or burn as it may well do when sautéing the odori. Also remember, as long as we're on garlic, the finer you chop it the more intensely it will flavor the dish. So, whole for less powerful, fine for intense.

John: Sorry, Patrick, I wasn't listening, as I was just reading a basic meat sauce recipe from Giuliano's master book in which he advises to chop the odori, "carrots, onion, celery, parsley, and garlic very fine …". For me, odori rule number one is to use fresh, not dried, herbs. Most markets these days carry fresh herbs year round. Buy them and use them when you need them. Dried herbs, in general are not worth using as they go stale and wind up tasting nothing like the real fresh thing.

I may also throw chives or small scallions into the herb category. And I would definitely include small, hot chilies dried or fresh if you want to "kick things up a notch". You can also grow herbs in your kitchen year round. And in more temperate climes, the hardier ones like rosemary and sage can grow outside year round. Basil too can be preserved in an airtight jar between layers of oil or kosher salt. If you feel like it, breathe a little carbon dioxide into your jar before closing. This rids the space of oxygen which blackens the herb. Don't keep fresh basil in a cold place, like your fridge. Also, as far as the intensity of garlic is concerned, if you want the full intensity , without chopping it up and having it become melded with the sauce, you can simply take a whole clove and lightly crush it with the side of a knife. This "ruptures" the cells that hold the garlicky essence, leaving the garlic whole to flavor the dish.

I will add a note here, though, on choosing either fresh or dried herbs for a particular dish:

🍽 Some herbs have a more pronounced flavor when they're dried than fresh, such as oregano. Consequently most of the time most recipes that call for oregano call for dried oregano. It's the other way around for herbs like basil and parsley. Herbs like thyme can go either way. Just keep this little tidbit and mind when you're creating your ideal version of your own recipe, and use what you think works best for you.

Patrick: If you can keep your fresh herbs growing then that is ideal. Unfortunately, fresh cut herbs do not have a long shelf life. So, if you don't plan on using them up through the week then they will end up in the compost. Therefore, dried herbs are useful and very often necessary. If you don't use them that often, then store in the freezer so they will not become bug ridden and stale.

John: *Garlic.* There shouldn't be much more to say about this subject, but there is. Garlic is probably the most pervasively, if not perversely, used flavoring in my kind of cooking. Unless you're trying to ward off werewolves, your husband, or a blind date, don't eat it raw. It needs to be cooked in some way. Typically you'll use it in a cooked dish. Or you might slice off the top part of a head, pour on a little olive oil, and roast it – to spread on toast or bread or pizza. Or you might use in a dressing of some kind like vinaigrette, or aioli. For these latter purposes the garlic should be "cooked" in a little salt and fresh lemon juice. But first a lesson in garlic preparation: To peel, smash (not squash) the clove *lightly* under the flat side of a chopping knife with your hand. Voila! The skin peels away easily.

To chop, slice roughly first with a large knife, then chop with a rocking motion of a large knife or a mezzaluna.

> 🍽 To puree, my favorite preparation, that I learned from Erick Vedel, is to take the peeled clove and rub it back and forth quickly across the tines at the end of a fork held firmly in a saucer containing a little lemon juice and salt. By the way, it's a waste of time, and diminishes the essence of the garlic to first remove the green "germ". I know most recipes recommend it, but it isn't necessary. But do it if you want.

Patrick: Garlic is also seen as very healthful to your body's system according to various articles written over time, and to my knowledge has never been disputed. Don't ask for the specifics of what it does for you because I don't recall off hand. Like the old common dictum, "shut up and eat your vegetables - they're good for you". You may want to try slicing a raw clove in half and rubbing the cut side against good toasted artisan style bread. By the way, when we refer to bread in this book, we are referring to artisan style bread, not the soft white or even whole grain style sandwich bread.

John: *Chilies.* Don't remove the seeds, as most recipes instruct. That's where the heat is! Wash you hands before, not just after, using the W/C.

Patrick: That brings back a memory when I think of how … well I laugh now, but not then! I was making a sauce once and crumbled some dried hot chilies by hand into it. Then I went to the bathroom, forgetting to wash my hands beforehand. You will soon learn that chilies have very hot oils that are released and will remain with you if you don't wash them off. I think you get my point! Also, as careful as you are about washing your hands, you may still feel their effects the next day unless your "system" has become used to them. Understand what I'm saying here? Good.

John: *Anchovies.* All right, not an herb or spice. But using them sparingly in certain dishes, can add to the overall result, without overpowering or insinuating itself as a stand-out ingredient. I prefer the larger anchovies which you can buy in many decent delis or markets, sold in bulk and preserved in salt. To prep for a recipe, hold the anchovy under cool running water, and while rinsing off the salt, carefully peel the fillets away from the spine with your thumbs. Wash away any guts or fins, and dry the fillets on paper towels.

You will rarely see whole anchovies left intact in a prepared dish (an exception being for example "Salad Niçoise"). Instead the fillets are often thrown whole into a cooking dish, where they will dissolve into the mixture. And if not used irrationally, they will add a special flavor that no one will be able to separately discern. As Julia Child might have said, "Who's to know?"

Patrick: I hate sardines, anchovies or any of that fishy stuff, so I have nothing to say on it except what I just did. If you too feel the same way, then you can probably omit them from a recipe as long as they are not the key base ingredient and not just producing a hint.

Spices

John: Though I said that odori included spices, I'm making them a separate section for several reasons, not the least of which is that these are typically dried items that keep reasonably well for longer periods of time in jars in your pantry (as opposed to herbs). If you are forced to buy spices in those ludicrously expensive little jars in the super market, then that's your fate. But if you can, and it's more possible these days in most places, buy them in the bulk section of a good market. Often times things that are usually sold pre-ground in those little jars, can be bought in bulk as whole seeds or pods, and you can grind them "fresh" yourself, as you need them. They keep better whole, and grinding them releases inner oils and what-not that make a more distinct impression on your dish. This is especially true of pepper corns, since pepper is so ubiquitous in most dishes. It's pretty common now for people to use fresh ground peppercorns at home. Doing it with other spices only makes sense, too. I keep a separate "burr" type of electric grinder for spices. Often times whole seeds or pods are warmed or toasted lightly in a dry skillet before grinding. This enhances their flavor even more.

John: *Pepper.* In my opinion, use black peppercorns. I have no idea why we need all these other colors.

Patrick: I agree. The others have their subtle properties, I suppose. But if you are going to use another color then let it be white for light color dishes where you want the flavor but not the appearance of black specs.

John: Mr. Finicky is all about appearances, folks.

Patrick: Not quite. Just ask anyone who has seen me. Anyway, there is a difference between the look of what you're cooking and the stylistic presentation. I like to refer to my pepper example as an aesthetic appearance of the food and not what Johnny prefers to do like paint pictures on plates with sauces, and create little tree landscapes with broccoli and all that nonsense.

John: Actually my presentations are very simple and unadorned. Patrick is just *trying* to be somewhat humorous.

Salt. It seems to me that all this stuff about grey, brown, orange, or yellow sea salt from France or New Zealand or wherever is a little over-reaching. I buy inexpensive ground sea salt in a regular round cardboard container for pouring into pots of cooking food. I buy a cheap large box of kosher salt for dumping into boiling water for cooking pasta or for brining meats, and I'll buy a course sea salt for grinding at the table when I want to have a fresher grind on my food when I'm eating it.

Patrick: Yeah, salt is salt basically. Something you need to understand is that if you are used to eating processed food, then you have unwittingly acquired a taste for salt and probably add more to the dishes you prepare than you should, which if you eat alone is fine but may turn out to be a flop with guests. I gave a friend some leftover something once and his comment was that it was good but needed salt. Well, I knew he was a processed food person so it took no sleuthing to figure out the issue did not lie with the dish I had given him. A while later I made a different dish that I stupidly made too salty - I could not eat it! An idea came to mind to give it to my friend as another "leftover". This time the reaction was quite different. Not only was it good but there was "just the right amount of salt."

John: Keep in mind that the Tuscans typically add a lot of salt to their cuisine. I'm not sure why. One anecdote I heard was that their bread, which is a staple, has no salt because it will keep longer, and that salting the rest of the food makes up for it. I also heard that being geographically located between the historical leading traders in salt (Genoa and Venice in the old, old days) gave the Florentines access to an excess of salt as they were always being bribed by one side to form an alliance against the other. So they used it copiously of course. I tend to use more salt than most other people like to taste in their food. It's what you get used to, as Patrick said. Anyway, other "odori", in no particular order are:

🍽 Star anise. It's one of those spices you've heard about, but until someone shoves it under your nose, you don't even think about using it. Erick Vedel shoved some under my nose, figuratively, by sticking one of the reddish-brown, dried, hard little starfish-looking things in a Provençal fish soup. Since then I find an excuse to put one into almost anything I'm making that's stew or soup-like, that requires some slow cooking. Its name implies, correctly, an anise flavor, but until you use it you'll never now how unique and mysterious it actually is. By the way, when you're done cooking, find the little dickens and remove it. It doesn't get soft or dissolve, and someone could crack a tooth on it.

🍽 Don't forget to remove bay leaves after cooking, too, or they could get stuck in someone's throat, unless you crush the leaf finely and remove the veins and stems.

Cumin, coriander (the seed, not the leaf, though it's the same plant), cardamom, nutmeg, cinnamon, cloves. You'll find these in Provencal, Moroccan, Tuscan, French, Spanish, and other cuisines. For example, the Italian version of béchamel, balsamella, often uses nutmeg, subtly. Nutmeg may also be found on cooked broccolini. Cumin may show up in a vinaigrette on grilled eggplant in Provence. Whole cloves buried in stews is not uncommon.

How about saffron, Spanish smoked paprika, or dried mustard? All add their own unique essence to appropriate dishes. Saffron is classic in a Milanese risotto. Smoked paprika is common in paellas. Dried mustard in vinaigrettes and other dressings for lettuce greens and other cooked or raw green vegetables.

Smoked jalapeños. I have to add here chipotles in adobo sauce, sold in Mexican markets in little cans. Like anchovies sparingly used, chipotles add a little smoky heat to sauces, soups, stews, and so forth. And "Who's to know?" Right, Julia? (God rest your soul).

Patrick: You should get to know these spices before experimenting with them. You can easily ruin a dish if you randomly throw something in because the moment moves you but you haven't a clue how it would work with the other ingredients. Playing with spices and herbs takes time. Experience them in established dishes before venturing blindly on your own.

John: Patrick is not the risk-taker of this dynamic duo. I like to throw stuff in and see if people can guess what it is. One final note on using herbs, spices, and other assorted odori:

> 🍽 *Some folks like to add them directly to the dish making them physically part of the sauce or stew itself. Sometimes, especially I've noticed in French and Provençal cooking, they're bundled up in cheese cloth together, or tied together with string. The bundled odori are removed prior to finishing the dish or eating it. I'm not aware of any hard and fast rule on this, unless you're trying to achieve a lighter, clearer broth or stock, which then would make sense.*

Patrick: My super risk taking days were long ago. John is trying to make up for lost time by using food as his risk vehicle. I think he likes to throw stuff in to see if people will run to the W/C. Some of his flop mystery ingredients have been grass clippings, driveway gravel and old sox, so please ask first before biting into one of his dishes upon a possible invite. Anyway, aside from aesthetics of the bundle, it also lets you control the amount of flavor you want to impart.

John: While we're still on the odori topic, tomatoes are also used as a flavoring when added sparingly to brighten a stock, or add color. I've also seen a whole onion thrown into a sauce or soup, then removed before serving. My daughter's mother-in-law, of Abruzzese heritage, like my brother and I, does this in her meat sauce for pasta. Maybe the poor Abruzzese needed to save the onion for another use, but the technique produces quite wonderful results.

Patrick: It is probably done to create a "clean" smooth sauce with the flavor of onion but not the solids of it. Believe it or not, some people love the flavor of certain things but not the consistency in a specific form. There's a thought to put in your pipe and smoke!

Olive Oil and Other Fats

John: Olive oils taste different depending on what kind of olives they're made from, where they're from, whether they're first pressings or not, the year they were made, who made them, how they were made, how ripe the olives were, and so on. Some are heavier tasting, some are fruitier, some are more acidic, etc. So it's up to your taste, your budget, and what your dish requires. But there's one thing I'm sure of that doesn't vary. The fresher the oil, the better it tastes. Paying top dollar for a "designer" oil doesn't make sense to me, not because it didn't start out as good quality oil, but because of its price it probably has been sitting on a retail shelf for a while waiting for some "gourmet chef" who wants to impress her friends to buy it. Supply and demand dictate that as price goes up, demand goes down. Lower demand literally means that fewer people buy less of it. Hence it doesn't turn on the retail shelf as quickly. Oil can go rancid, get stale and taste just yucky if it's kept too long, in too much light, and in too warm a place. My theory is that if you find a good quality, inexpensive oil that appears to sell in great volume, then you'll probably end up with a fresher oil, on the whole. So, I buy stuff from Trader Joe's for $6.99 per liter, because they make and sell a ton of that stuff and the stock turns rapidly. Of course I use a lot, too.

Patrick: I agree. Unless you live in olive oil territory or the bottle has the date of the pressing, then avoid the specialty stores offering and go with good quality where there is good turnover.

John: Don't use olive oil to fry stuff at high temperatures. Use canola, or peanut, or corn oil. Maybe using a little olive oil in the frying mixture adds some flavor, while raising the overall smoking point. That's why you'd use a little oil with butter if you want to fry in butter, since butter's burning or smoking point is quite low.

Patrick: For general, non-deep fat, high-heat frying, go with the canola for health reasons, or peanut for necessary flavor.

John: As far as I'm concerned there are very few reasons to want to deep fry at home. It's messy, it's dangerous, it smells up the house, and it's an expensive cooking medium. And rarely do things turn out the way you want them, unless you do a lot of deep fat frying and are really adept at it. To sate my craving for "pomme fritte" I'll go to a good restaurant that does them well. There are some things I do fry, but I will get to those dishes later. And if you have the need to eat an oil-cooked potato more frequently, I like to roast slices or wedges in a rosemary olive oil coating in a hot oven. Salt them when you're done and eat hot.

Patrick: I do not do much deep frying either, but I do fry things. Deep frying is not high on my list of preferred cooking techniques simply because whether done right or wrong, the end product retains too much grease for my liking.

John: For that matter, let's talk about oils and fats a little bit in general. Adding pancetta or a chunk off the end of a prosciutto to dried beans when they're cooking, or as a good tasting fat to finish cooking braised greens in, is a great idea. Simply using olive oil all the time to sauté or braise can get a little boring and you miss out on the other fat flavors in your cooking. You don't have to eat the chunk of leftover ham, fatback, or salt pork when you're done. Give it to the dog. He'll appreciate it, and *he* won't worry about his cholesterol.

Patrick: This technique of added meat fat is especially good for dishes that do not have meat as part of their makeup. It is just like throwing a ham bone into your American style bean soup.

John: Now on the subject of butter as a cooking fat, generally I don't cook with that much with it. It is a treat, though, and you should use it as much as you like, for appropriate dishes. I usually save my butter allotment for pastries, or to munch on a chuck of fresh baguette while I'm cooking dinner or with my coffee in the morning. I usually save my heavy cream intake for dessert toppings as well, though it has ample, wonderful uses in main dishes. Just remember to not whip your cream too stiff for your dessert topping. Let it ooze a little over the edges of your tart tatin. Don't add sugar or flavorings. Good fresh cream is good in its own right. Like all good, elemental foods, treat it with respect.

Patrick: I don't know about you but I have no idea what a "tart tatin" is. Probably one of his French dishes. I keep the butter handy on the counter at all times. It is necessary for my bread, toast, sautéing mushrooms, onions, and so forth. I ain't scared of it since I don't eat it like it's a chocolate bar. I don't consider it a treat but more of a staple. Wonder why he is so careful about allotting his butter after his little quote he borrowed from Julia Childs about Americans being scared to eat, or something like that. I think he's "yella'"! Not sure where the whipped cream fits into this butter segment, but he is older and wiser so he must know the reason.

John: Actually my mantra is that one should be able to eat anything, in moderation and within a balanced diet. In case, dear reader, you haven't noticed by now, Patrick's role is not accuracy, but "comic" relief.

Patrick: Bingo! Does he think people will be able to sit through his dissertations without my rest stops?

Some Other Basic Things To Know

John: *Fish.* Buy fresh fish from a place that sells a lot of fish. Otherwise don't bother. Fish is good for you, tastes great, and adds a host of dishes to your repertoire. So find a good place to buy it, and learn to cook your favorite fish dishes well. Fish can be tricky, and each fish has its own idiosyncrasies, so focus on a few kinds. The main exception to the fresh fish rule, is salt cod or baccala. Dried salt cod was a staple for eons, since fresh fish doesn't keep well. Armies traveled on salt cod, and some early international trade was based on it. Though it's hard to find these days, learn its wonders and have a couple of dishes in your arsenal.

Eggs. Like every other kind of basic food product, buy the freshest and be willing to pay for it. Organic, cage-free produced eggs from a local farm are better by far. The yolks are yellow and stand up like a hemisphere. Better eggs are also very important in the quality of fresh made pasta, pastries, frittatas, and aioli – not just for frying, poaching, coddling, or boiling.

Pasta. If you're going to make your own lasagna or stuffed pastas, then make your own egg pasta. Even if it's available in your market's cooler or from a fresh pasta store, it's never as thin, elastic, or fresh as if you made it yourself.

Sauces and dressings. Make your own pasta sauces and salad dressings. As far as salad dressings go, I'd stick with simple, clean-tasting variants of the basic vinaigrette. For the real quality of the salad, focus on the quality of the greens your using. Don't make up for crappy lettuce by smothering it with gobs of ranch dressing from a bottle. And pasta dishes are about the pasta, its freshness, how it's cooked, its shape, its texture. The sauce enhances and works with the pasta. Heavy, tomatoey canned sauces with "powdered onion and garlic, natural and artificial flavors, sodium benzoate to preserve freshness, etc." are not to be tolerated in *your* kitchen! Light sauces, and not too much, make pastas shine, they don't smother them to death.

Tomatoes. Buy the best quality canned tomatoes. If you can, grow your own heirlooms, like for instance the always dependable "Costoluto Genovese", for both sauces and eating raw. With excess harvest, simply halve the tomatoes and simmer for hours in their own juice with a little salt. Add no water. When it's thick enough to suit you, then put it through a food mill, and freeze it in yogurt containers, for Winter's use. Don't ever buy commercial tomatoes in your store's produce section. These are bred to travel well, not to eat. Unless a local farmer is raising heirlooms and selling them at a local market. I'm basically saying not to buy, eat, or cook fresh tomatoes, out of season. I think tomatoes are unique in this way.

Patrick: John is just trying to scare the hell out of everybody, and you'll think you might as well put the book down because you don't a have chicken farm next door, a brook in your back yard stocked with trout, or a garden full of your own tomatoes. Don't panic, it is OK to use non-farm fresh eggs and non-local tomatoes. When you can find heirloom tomatoes, fine, but when you can't, that's fine, too. Dried pasta is essential to certain dishes just as fresh is essential to others. Typically, machines are set up to prepare lasagna sheets, spaghetti shaped, and fettuccine style fresh pastas. I use mine for sheets and strips only. I make lasagnas and ravioli with the sheets, and use the strip cutter for fettuccine style dishes. As far as the sauces and dressings: salad dressings homemade are best but if you want an out of the bottle dressing or are in a pinch, find yourself a top notch one to keep on hand for when you need to cheat a little bit. Sauces should always be used sparingly as an accent to the dish, not as a blanket to cover it up. A sure sign of a dumpy Italian restaurant for example is that their veal parmigiano is buried beneath a glop of cheese and a one size fits all sauce. You don't want to eat that and you certainly don't want to make it.

John: Patrick is worth his culinary weight in gold, if all he does is keep me honest, folks. Though he can be a royal pain in the butt. And he would probably say the same about me. The pain in the butt part, I mean. But I do agree with his "Royal-Pain-In-The-Assness" that one should not be limited to the "ideal" ingredients. What I do argue for is getting the best that you can, because that's what makes your food that best that it can be.

Appetizers

John: This is a short lesson, as it basically is all about what you'd like to snack on while you're cooking, or serving your guests while they're standing around getting in the way while you cook.

Patrick: I try to stay away from eating anything when cooking. You will be taste testing as you go along and that is sufficient. Besides, Johnny is either talking about appetizers or snacking. They are two different things. Appetizers are a lead-in to the meal, usually light and small. Snacks are things eaten anytime during the day or night. I think people are beginning to understand John is not doing the book on his own. I still need to hold his hand.

John: He's right. Some people like loud music when they work, for example. I guess I need his constant irritation to do the fine writing that I turn out.

Here's what I like (for *appetizers,* Patrick!)

Good, un-pitted olives. Find a good deli and buy a variety that you like. Put them out at room temp, with a pit bowl next to them.

Baguette with or without butter. Tear off chunks with you hands and eat. Or dip into olive oil.

Cheeses. Always at room temperature - with or without bread.

Bruschetta. This, by the way, is pronounced "bruce – ketta". Not "brooshetta". If you go to an Italian restaurant where the waiters pronounce it wrong, leave immediately. Or if they don't correct you when *you* pronounce it wrong.

Small, thin slices of baguette, toasted lightly, and maybe rubbed with a peeled garlic clove.

- Chop some fresh tomato and basil together, all some salt and pepper, and spread on the bread.
- Simply drizzle on some olive oil.
- Make a pate of chopped chicken livers, sautéed in some chopped onion and oil, flavored with some parsley. Salt and pepper.
- Some peperonata.
- Anchovies or anchovy paste, maybe with a squirt of lemon, or some capers, chopped olives, or strips of roasted red peppers.
- Cooked (or canned) cannellini, pureed with roasted garlic, and olive oil.
- Etc.

Patrick: You'll notice he's into this baguette thing. While good in its own right, I find them a bit whimpy. If you want good bruschetta then use good Italian bread. (See the recipe for "Pane di Napoleone" on page 47).

Pinzamonio (literally, "finger food")

John: Fresh vegetables, *especially* fennel, cut into sticks and dipped into very fresh olive oil, liberally doused with salt and pepper.

Marinated herring

Buy in a deli or deli section of a good market

Herring in sour cream sauce

Again, a good deli item.

Grilled Bread and Cheese on Skewers

- Cut chunks of good solid artisan bread, and some fresh mozzarella.
- Thread them on skewers.
- Brush with olive oil.
- Sprinkle on salt and pepper.
- Grill.

Prosciutto and Fresh Figs

Prosciutto and Fresh Melon

Sliced Assorted Cured Meats and Salames

Shave some Parmigiano on the platter, too.

Patrick: Nice. This is probably another good spot to interject something that separates the two of us. Johnny seems to always be in the "restaurant" mode. A bit more formal than myself, and probably has a tendency to brandish something fancy with a bit of flair. I on the other hand, tend to only offer rustic simple casualness. The conversation is loose, friendly, a little confrontational, sometimes caustic and even disrespectful, but always honest. However, the food is expected to be appreciated and acknowledged. Not doing so is an insult within my home and guests will not be asked to return. I'm a nice warm and fuzzy guy, ain't I?

John: Pat is all that, folks. I keep him around because he is a good cook, and cares about his food – more than most people do. That's what we share. But I have to say, he is not nearly as obnoxious as he may appear to you, our treasured reader.

Patrick: Our treasured reader? You bought the book already you'd think he'd drop the sales hype.

Bread and Pizza

John: Bread may be the staff of life, but pizza is the only yeasted dough I usually bake at home. Though I have a genuine restaurant gas range with an oven that can get quite hot, and some really heavy duty terra cotta tiles that I scammed from a mason who was throwing them away when he was done working on a restaurant job, baking yeasted bread doughs at home never ever re-creates the same thing as what you get at a good artisan bakery or good restaurant that has the right high-temp baking equipment, wood-fired, gas, or otherwise.

> *If you go to France or Italy, for example, people buy their bread at bakeries, on their way home from work. That's why I can never understand why most cookbooks, even this one for some dumb reason, typically have a "Bread" chapter. Probably you couldn't get the damn book past the publisher if you didn't.*

The only other bread I make is a classic Tuscan loaf of bread, because you can't find it in the States, or outside of Tuscany for that matter. Tuscan bread works best for making certain recipes, like panzanella, or eating with certain soups, like ribollita, because Tuscan bread is dense, has no salt, and keeps for a long, long time unwrapped on your kitchen counter. Making bread at home is no substitute for a good bakery made artisan loaf. And while I am lucky enough in Portland, Oregon to have access to multiple artisanal bakeries, many of you, including Patrick, do not. This idea taken from the *New York Times* November 8, 2006 issue, is the brainchild of Jim Lahey, and the results are remarkable!

> *I have told you already that this book will most typically not list specific amounts for ingredients, or give overly explicit cooking directions, because all that is for you to experiment with. It forces you to think about what you're doing instead of reading instructions, it requires you to make mistakes, and it enables you to learn from your mistakes. Having said that, all baking normally requires more specificity because baking is typically more "chemical" in nature, with ingredients interacting with one another in the cooking process to produce a new entity.*

Here's the original recipe, followed by Patrick's experimental rendition. He now has a true artisanal baker in his community. Him!

Jim Lahey's No-Knead Bread

INGREDIENTS: 3 cups flour, ¼ teaspoon instant yeast, 1 ¼ teaspoons salt..

- Combine ingredients in a big bowl.
- Add 1-5/8 cups of water and stir just until well-blended (the dough will be "shaggy" and sticky).
- Cover bowl with plastic and let rest for at least 12 hours. (dough's surface should be bubbly).
- Flour a work surface and dump the dough on it.
- Fold dough over on itself a couple of times, cover with plastic, and let rest 15 minutes.
- Coat a towel well with flour.
- Flouring your hands lightly, form dough into a large ball and put onto the floured towel.
- Cover with another floured towel and let rise until doubled – about 2 hours.
- In the meantime put a 6-8 quart heavy covered pot (say an enameled Dutch oven) into a cold oven and heat oven to 450F.
- Carefully turn dough into hot pot (the dough will look messy), put on cover, and bake for 30 minutes.
- Remove lid and bake another 15-30 minutes until browned and crusty.
- Cool on a rack.

Patrick's "Pane di Napoleone"

The original recipe, above, has created quite a culinary stir. That is to say for example, people are going out to buy expensive pots to bake the bread in. Through my experimentation I have found no pots are necessary. You gotta have good bricks for your oven though. I am not crazy about those polymer pizza style stones out there. But if that's all you have then use it. I have tried the original recipe, and although acceptable, I needed to alter to my personal standards. Therefore I have experimented in various ways with it to achieve a bread that I am totally satisfied with. I am not easy to please where bread is concerned. I prefer an elongated loaf as opposed to the typical round Tuscan shape. But if you want the round shape then just shape it that way during the shaping process.

INGREDIENTS FOR 1 LOAF: 2 Cups bread flour, 1 Cup regular flour, 1-5/8 C warm water, 1 tsp honey, 1 tsp salt, 1 tsp yeast regular yeast.

- In a large, deep bowl add the water, yeast and honey and stir together.
- Add the salt and stir some more.
- Add the flours and mix all together.
- The dough should be more wet than dry, but it should pull away from the sides of the bowl and start to form a rough ball.
- If not, then add a little more bread flour until it does.
- Next cover the bowl with a towel and a large enough lid being careful the towel does not touch the dough.
- Put the bowl in a draft free spot and let sit *at least 15 hours.*
- After this time remove the lid and towel and you should see a bubbly mass.
- Now sprinkle some flour around the edges of the dough where it meets the bowl and a little on the top. Doing this will help keep the dough from sticking to the bowl when removing it to a well floured board.
- With a small paddle or cake batter style rubber spatula, start freeing up the dough from the bowl by working around the entire perimeter.
- As you do this, start tipping the bowl and continue scraping the bowl to free the dough until the dough falls out onto a floured board.
- Flour your hands and using a pastry blade very carefully fold the dough over a few times to make a ball.
- Do *not* do any typical kneading. Maybe 20 seconds of just folding and forming a ball is all you will need.
- Sprinkle some flour into the same bowl you used before. No need to clean the bowl first.
- Place the ball of dough back into the bowl and cover again with the towel and top as before.
- Set in draft free spot and let set for *at least 3 hours.*
- Now you are ready to prepare the dough for the baking stage.
- Using the prior technique mentioned above for removing the dough from the bowl, empty it with the smoother side up on a well floured board.
- You *must* handle the dough very gently from here on until it goes into the oven.
- Flour your hands and using your pastry blade gently shape the dough from the edges into an elongated shape approximately 12" long. Absolutely do *not* work the dough from the top.

- Cover with a towel.
- Put your pizza bricks or pizza stone in the oven and preheat to 500F.
- When your oven has reached the temperature you are now ready to transfer the dough to the oven.
- Using your pastry blade free the dough up carefully from the board.
- If it is sticking in places move some flour under it using the blade.
- When it is free, put the blade under one section of the dough and grab the other end with your other hand, pick it up and quickly transfer to the hot stone in the oven.
- Very quickly fix its shape a little on the stones.
- Cover with an aluminum foil "tent" and close the door. Let bake for 30 minutes. Do *not* open the oven.
- After 30 minutes, remove the foil and let bake another 10-15 minutes until nicely browned.
- Remove from the oven and let rest on its edge to cool.
- Do not cut for at least one hour. Best served after at least 2 hours. The texture should be nice and airy inside and crusty outside.
- Be sure to store once completely cooled in a paper bag.

John: Whew!

The dough after first mixing

Risen for 18 hours

Turning dough onto floured board

Shaping

Placed on pre-heated oven bricks

Tented with foil

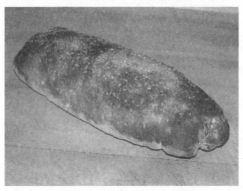

A crusty, chewy, airy Artisanal loaf

This same dough can be used for pizza. For thin pizza, divide the dough in half. For thicker, work with the dough in it's original size. You will still go through the 2 rising process.

- On a well-floured board gently kneed it out to a small fat but flat shape. Dust with flour as necessary.
- Let rest a few minutes and begin to press out to a bigger and thinner shape.
- Let rest and repeat. You will want to flip the dough over to make sure it is not sticking and keep things floured. You don't want a really wet dough here.
- If you have the ability then you can begin to spin the dough in the air and work the edges to get your final thickness and size.
- Let rest, covered with a towel until oven is at 500 degrees. This takes practice, as does anything.

John: It's been drilled into our little foodie heads that yeasted dough requires kneading to develop the wheat's gluten so that the dough becomes stretchy, allowing the yeast's fermentation to produce bubbles that create expansion. As it turns out, time resting can replace the kneading process, and holding in the moisture during baking completes the technique. That said, here's my pizza dough recipe for the traditionalists out there.

John's Pizza Dough

I will never stop experimenting with my pizza dough, though I think I'm getting closer and closer to what I'm striving for.

INGREDIENTS: Flour, water, salt, yeast, oil.

- For each 1-2 person pizza, put one cup of filtered water into a heavy glass bowl and microwave it until the water is quite warm, but not hot.
- Dissolve about a teaspoon of sugar in the water.
- Sprinkle about a half teaspoon of yeast over the surface of the water.
- Let the yeast dissolve itself into the water and form a foamy "head" (about 15 minutes let's say).
- Start stirring in plain, unbleached white bread or all-purpose flour and a little salt a little at a time with a heavy wooden spoon. Do not use cake flour.
- Add a very little olive oil at this point, if you wish.
- As each half cup or so of floor is incorporated, and the dough gets sticky, add a little more flour.
- When the dough no longer gets really sticky, but before it's too dry, turn the dough out onto a floured wooden board.
- Knead by folding the top half of the floppy circle of dough toward you for form a semi-circle, then vigorously push the dough down and away with your palms.
- Turn the dough 90 degrees on the board and repeat the folding, kneading movement.
- Keep doing this for a few minutes (working a little flour from time to time) until the dough is not too sticky, but not dry – and remains light and not too dense and heavy.
- Put it back into the bowl, put some plastic wrap over the bowl, and a dish towel over the plastic wrap.
- Let it sit and rise for an hour or more, or overnight. There's no rush. Let the gluten work.
- Punch it down.
- Scoop it out of the bowl with your hands.
- Knead it lightly into a very smooth ball.
- Let it rest and rise again under a floured dish towel.
- Flatten the dough with you fingers and palms. Sometimes I use a rolling pin, which I've seen a lot in Provence.
- Put it on a pizza peel lightly dusted with a little flour and/or some fine cornmeal.
- Add toppings.
- Sometimes I'll bake it very lightly before I put the toppings on, just to firm the dough up a little.

You must bake pizza at the highest temperature your oven will reach, and you must use heavy tiles to bake it on. Be sure to pre-heat the tiles as the oven is heating. You want the edges of the dough to be very crusty, even charred a little.

A Classic Provençal Pizza (Pissaladiere)

INGREDIENTS: Onions, anchovies, fresh Roma tomatoes (they are less watery), garlic, un-pitted olives.

- Sautee sliced onions in some olive oil. Set aside.
- Sauté some anchovies and garlic lightly in some olive oil in another skillet until you have a paste.
- Slice some fresh tomatoes very, very thin with a very sharp knife.
- Spread the anchovy/garlic paste on the flattened, uncooked pizza dough.
- Scatter the onions over next.
- Lay the tomatoes over the whole pizza only one layer thick.
- Strategically place a few un-pitted green and/or black olives in top.
- Bake.

The Italian Classic – if there is such a thing

- Spread a light tomato sauce, flavored with a little garlic and basil over the dough.
- Strew some very thin slices of fresh mozzarella over the top.
- Add some salt.
- Bake.

My Grandson's Favorite

- Spread some good Italian sliced pepperoni over the cheese before you bake.

Sicilian – at least my rendition

INGREDIENTS: Olive oil, tomato sauce, garlic, anchovies, capers, fresh mozzarella.

- Put some olive oil in the bottom of a rectangular cookie sheet, and spread it around with your hands.
- Put the dough in the middle of the pan and stretch and form the dough to fit the pan. (Keep your hands oily).
- Cover the pan lightly with some waxed or parchment paper and let the dough rise.
- Spread a tomato sauce flavored with garlic and anchovies over the dough. Sauté the anchovies and garlic first into a paste, then add the tomato puree and simmer.
- Put capers on top of the sauce.
- Bake until almost done.
- Add sliced or shredded mozzarella.
- Finish baking until the cheese bubbles.
- Cut into squares.

Focacce and Schiacciate
(Focaccia and schiacciata in the singular)

These two flat breads are cooked like the Sicilian pizza above. It is dough that is spread out on an oily, rectangular, rimmed cookie sheet. Covered with parchment or plastic wrap and a towel and left to rise. Then baked. You can find specific recipes for focacce and schiacciatte, but like pizza (which however is cooked directly on heated bricks in the oven) just about anything goes as far as flavorings and toppings. Here are some ideas off the top of my head:

- Make the dough, letting it rise at least twice, using oil, lard, or butter as the shortening.
- Add to the dough while mixing one or more of:
    1. rendered bits of pancetta
    2. chopped oil-cured black olives
    3. chopped fresh rosemary (and/or other herbs)
    4. caramelized onions
    5. roasted garlic cloves
    6. very coarsely ground sea salt

Or sprinkle bits of the above on the top before baking. There is a recipe I've seen that urges you to strew some fresh grapes on top of one layer of dough, then place another layer of dough on that and seal the edges, spread more grapes and oil on top, and then bake. Or you could use this "sandwich" method with ingredients other than grapes.

Patrick: Pizzas are all about the dough and when cooked, the crust. If that isn't right then it doesn't matter what you put on it, its worthless. Off course many so called pizzerias manage to screw up both, but surprisingly enough they remain in business. I am not sure this is because most people don't know what good pizza tastes like, or they just don't care. And to make matters worse, delivered pizza makes a bad pizza even more horrible. And it still gets eaten. I have yet to find a good pizzeria in Connecticut. I have tried the so called "best", and they were just average to me.

Sauces

John: Here I'll discuss sauces of various ilks, including the type that may be put on pastas and polenta. But I'll also talk about some basic sauce-like concoctions like aioli, balsamella, and reductions (or "gravies"). However, like the rest of the book, I'm not even attempting to cover all the basic recipes, but simply to talk about a few variations on some essential themes so that you can use them as a take-off point from which to explore your own ideas. Most of this will deal with pasta type sauces. I eschew a lot of French style cooking which depend heavily on sauces, whether it's a Hollandaise for say asparagus, or a cream sauce for poached fish. I could be accused of being very Italian and Provençal oriented in my choices of recipe themes, but it's really because that's the style I find the most clean, fresh, and honest in its straightforwardness. So it's just personal bias, but one I think could be a bias that more people might begin to follow for health, simplicity of preparation, and general lightness and freshness of attitude. Dried pasta (e.g. spaghetti, penne, orechiette, conchiglie, etc.) typically requires something to enhance and combine with to make a dish. Of course this is also true of dishes made from fresh egg noodle type pastas.

A little immigrant history here first. It was typical for each wave of ethnic immigration that the young or American born children of those that came off the boats wanted to assimilate into the entrenched "American" culture as soon as they could. Basically this allowed them to escape the bigotry and racism that the prior ethnic immigrant groups heaped on them. And for young people especially, becoming part of "the crowd" has always been important. So for instance, as I explained earlier, my mother and her sisters passed themselves off as French. And though only Italian was spoken in their home and indeed in the whole neighborhood, the four would never speak Italian outside their "'hood". To this day my mother can sing little songs in Italian she learned as a little girl, but she can't speak a word of Italian – except to name the foods they ate, in Abruzzese dialect. So, continuing this lengthy point I'm trying to make, almost all Italian immigrants came from the south of Italy, traditionally the very poorest regions (e.g. Sicily, Abruzzo, Calabria, etc.). They came here, like most immigrants do and have always done, because they were poor! But once they got here, they started building the myth, outside their ghetto communities, that they were from "Northern Italy", which was the wealthier, more pedigreed region. Better to be accepted by the growing middle class Irish-Americans, German-Americans, blueblood English-Americans, and so forth. To this day, you will still hear descendents of these first Calabrese, Abruzzese, and Siciliani repeat the myth that their grandparents, or great-grandparents came from "Rome" or "the north". But their dialects and the food they still eat betray them. Mozzarella is "mootzarell", Pasta e' fagioli is "pasta fazool", and they drop all the final vowels like Willie Brown always dropped his final "g's". So to pursue this little history lesson to the food issue, what these poor people ate basically was pasta. The adornment was a little meat sauce (and I mean a **little**), a little garlic and oil, maybe with some scraps of carbonized bacon, a little grated cheese, and an egg broken into the hot bowl of pasta, maybe a few clams and a little white wine and oil. Like the food of all poor cultures, meat for example was a "condiment", sauce was a flavoring, but the pasta was the dish. And so, if you want to cook pasta right, you use the best pasta and you flavor it oh so carefully with something that will never, ever assault the pasta's claim to the seat of pre-eminence.

A "Bolognese"

This is my version of a Bolognese-style pasta sauce.

INGREDIENTS: Lean beef, prosciutto (optional), carrot, celery, onion, garlic, parsley, tomatoes (or puree), red wine, dried porcini, broth.

- Take a chunk of inexpensive lean beef and chop, dice, of snip it with shears into small bits. I adamantly refuse to grind the meat or use ground beef.
- Brown it lightly in some oil. Here you may also add some chopped prosciutto.
- Add some finely diced odori (I use a food processor and "pulse" so as not to produce a puree) carrot, celery, onion, garlic, and parsley. Sauté lightly.
- Add some chopped, peeled, and seeded tomatoes (or tomato puree, or a little paste) and blend into the other ingredients.
- Pour in some red wine and simmer off some of the alcohol.
- Add some chopped dried porcini mushrooms which have soaked in some warm water, along with the soaking water.
- Add some broth if necessary.
- Add salt and pepper.
- Cover tightly.
- Simmer very low for a long, long time (i.e. hours).
- Once it's cooked, you can adjust the seasoning, and the viscosity by simmering away some of the liquid or adding more broth.

Cooking and saucing pasta

- Boil pasta in well-salted water. No one knows what "al dente" really means, but you never want the pasta to be flaccid, or mushy, or water-logged.
- When done, pour some of the cooking water into the serving bowl to warm it and a little into a separate bowl to use as a "thinner", if necessary.
- Drain the pasta, but do no rinse it.
- Put the pasta back into the cooking pot.
- Add some sauce and mix lightly.
- Keep adding small amounts, and mixing, until the pasta is lightly coated, but not hidden, suffocated, drowned, or smothered.
- Warm it up a little over a low flame if you want to.
- Check the thickness/thinness of the sauce, and add some cooking water if necessary, to please you. It should not be gummy or too thick.
- Empty the hot water from the serving bowl, and dump the sauced pasta into it.

- Serve.
- Allow people to grate their own parmigiano onto their own servings if they want.

🍽 *By the way, I've found in Italy especially, and in Provence, for example, dishes are often **not** served piping hot. More and more these days my wife and I are eating food closer to room temperature. The benefits to this are that you can taste the food better since it's not scalding your tongue, the flavors have a chance to meld a little while the dish is cooling off a bit, and you don't have to time your preparations so that everything arrives hot on the table at the same time. Exceptions to this are for example, deep-fried foods, but I don't cook or eat these anyway so it's a moot (not "mute") point.*

Chicken Parmigiano

Patrick: A staple in many Italian/American households, this dish, although simple, can be screwed up very easily as no doubt you may have experienced in many so-called Italian restaurants where you find it swimming in sauce and cheese. Done properly, the breaded cutlets are tender, moist and flavorful. I learned the basic cutlet technique from an old Italian/American man in the kitchen of a local deli many, many years ago. With the careful addition of sauce and cheese it becomes a dish fit for a special dinner or a simple meal with the family. I will only give you the recipe for the breaded cutlets here as well as putting it together. The preferred sauce is a basil/tomato (see page 63) or you can choose one of your preferences.

INGREDIENTS: Chicken breasts (skinned and boned), bread crumbs (unseasoned), egg, milk, salt, pepper.

- Each side of the breast can be cut into half or thirds diagonally, with the grain, depending on the size. A breast is considered whole when both sides are attached. Therefore one side of a chicken breast is known as ½ chicken breast. You cut them to bring into easily workable sizes.
- Each piece is pounded out thin between sheets of waxed or parchment paper. Too thin and they will dry out and toughen!. They will at least double in size after you pound them out.
- Dredge each piece in a mixture of egg and a little milk. Let the bulk drain off when removing.
- Dredge each piece in the bread crumbs. As you do this, press the crumbs into the meat with your finger tips as if you were working bread dough. After both sides of the cutlet have been breaded, gently shake off loose crumbs. Lay the breaded cutlets in a dish or refrigerator storage receptacle.
- When you have finished breading all the cutlets, wrap the dish in plastic wrap, or put the top on the storage type ware and refrigerate for at least three hours. This allows the coating to "cure" and adhere well to the meat.
- Fry each cutlet in about ½" inch canola (preferred) oil to a light golden brown on each side. You don't want them to get dark brown. I use an old fashioned electric skillet with the temperature control on the handle, but you can also do this on the stove top.
- Drain on paper towels.
- To put the dish together, put a little sauce on the bottom of a glass baking dish and coat evenly. Line the bottom with the cutlets. Do not layer them. If you have more cutlets than the dish will hold then use another dish or freeze the extra for future use.
- Sprinkle freshly grated Parmigiano-Reggiano cheese on the cutlets. Cover but do not hide the cutlets with thinly sliced fresh mozzarella cheese.
- Now add the sauce to the top but do not "bury" the cutlets in it. Add a few more randomly placed pieces of fresh mozzarella on top of the sauce.
- Bake uncovered in a medium degree oven until the cheese melts and everything is heated through.
- Remove from oven and let rest before serving.

John: Unfortunately, Patrick doesn't realize that this is the "Sauce" section. But we'll let it pass for now, since it is a really good recipe. And the following recipe is a good one, too, though a tad "odd".

"Meatballs, Y' Bastard"

Patrick: First let me explain the name. My brother wanted me to send him my recipe for the longest time and I kept delaying my response. His repeated emails to me to request it finally generated this response from me. Here in all its glory is my original recipe that I emailed him with the subject heading, "meatballs y' bastard".

John: I need to note here that the "bastard" that Pat is referring to is *me*. A pet name that connotes affection, I'm sure.

> **⦿ Pat's Note:** *I created and mastered this recipe over time with much trial and error. If you think it easy to find great meatballs wherever you go, then fagetaboudit! Everything is "about" in measurement, y' bastard!*

INGREDIENTS: Ground beef, pork and veal, eggs, fennel, bread crumbs, parsley, mint, basil, pepper, parmigiano and fontinella, garlic oil (crushed garlic cloves soaked in olive oil).

Now pay attention, y' bastard!

- Put the meat, egg, crumbs, parsley, mint, fennel, pepper, oil and cheeses in a bowl and mix well with your hands.
- Add just enough water until the mixture is very moist but not falling apart dripping wet, (this is critical and will take trial and error until you've done it a few times,).
- Now, roll the meat gently into balls (do not pack like an ice ball you're going to throw into the side of someone's head).
- Then roll in some bread crumbs and place on oiled baking sheet.
- Bake until done, turning once or twice.
- Any remaining cook time will be done in the sauce.
- If it turns out like crap, then it means I forgot something, and that's just tough luck, and you will have to figure it out yourself.

Suggested sauce: Bolognese- style

Suggested pasta: Imported Italian dried spaghetti

John: Hey, Patrick, y' bastard, at least give Grampa some credit here. I'm sure you heard him whispering in your ear when you were "perfecting" this meatball recipe. This is the closest anyone's gotten to Grampa's original.

Puttanesca

John: Without daring to make a literal translation of this term here, suffice it to say it's a bold, deep, and spirited concoction that is one of my son-in-law's favorites He claims his Italian heritage is "Roman". This is my version, and not necessarily "the classic".

INGREDIENTS: Olive oil, garlic, anchovy fillets, tomato paste, capers, un-pitted olives, hot chili pepper flakes, dried pasta.

- Pour lots of olive oil into a deep skillet, and heat it up You'll need to use more than you think you should.
- Add some chopped garlic and sauté a little tiny bit.
- Add some anchovy fillets. I use quite a few. "Melt" them by stirring in the warm oil until they disintegrate.

> 🍽 **Anchovy note:** Anchovies in oil or salt in a jar, or from a tin are OK. But if you can find a place that sells them bulk, preserved in and coated with salt, that's lot better. If you use the former, just throw the whole fillet into the skillet with the garlic. If you the latter, you need to peel the fillets off each side of the fish skeleton with your fingers while rinsing them under cold running water. Dry them off before you throw them into the oil.

- Add some tomato paste. I use a lot. Stir and "fry" the paste in the hot oil for several minutes, making an oily, tomatoey, garlicky, anchovy mess.
- Add some hot water, a little at a time, stirring constantly until you reach the consistency you want. (Alternatively, use an unseasoned tomato puree instead of paste and water).
- Add hot pepper flakes. The sauce should be spicy.
- Add capers.
- Add black olives that you pit and slice yourself.
- Add some pepper and salt, if you don't think the anchovies are giving the sauce enough saltiness. Remember this is a sauce of strong, distinct flavors.
- Sauce the cooked pasta as above. Usually it's spaghetti, for what it's worth.

No cheese!

Carbonara

INGREDIENTS: Garlic, pancetta, olive oil, hot pepper flakes, eggs, parmigiano, dried spaghetti.

- Start boiling the pasta water when you start the sauce because the hot sauce needs to go onto the hot pasta right before serving. Neither should sit around waiting for the other. Usually the pasta is spaghetti.
- Chop up some garlic and pancetta, or salt pork, but not American style bacon unless of course you want a smoky flavor.
- Put the garlic and pancetta into a pot with oil, salt, and some hot pepper flakes. This dish doesn't need to be too, too spicy.
- "Carbonize" or brown the pancetta well, until all of its fat is rendered into the olive oil.
- While the pancetta is carbonizing, and the pasta is close to been cooked, beat some eggs together with some parmigiano.
- Drain the pasta and immediately dump it into a warmed bowl.
- Immediately pour over the hot oil/pancetta mixture and toss.
- Immediately then pour the egg/cheese mixture onto the pasta and toss. (the hot pasta cooks the egg as it coats the pasta).
- Serve at once.
- Encourage diners to grind lots of pepper onto their pasta.

Patrick: We need to be a bit specific about the amount of egg used. Basically, one beaten egg per ½ lb pasta. And incidentally, I prefer bucatini as opposed to spaghetti. When the mixing is completed there should not be any "soupyness" in the bottom of the bowl if done properly. I also leave the garlic whole and do not chop. The oil and garlic I use is from my bottle of the combination of the two that I always have marinating, available as needed.

John: See what I mean? He can't leave well enough alone!

Patrick: Nor should anyone else. That's the point of the book! Sorry, I forgot, since he is older he tends to forget where he's going, so every once in a while I am the roadmap that needs to be flashed in front of him.

The Classic Parma Sauces (especially for fresh pastas)

- Melted butter, grated parmigiano, salt and pepper.
- Melted butter, grated parmigiano, breadcrumbs, salt and pepper.
- Melted butter, cream, ground walnuts, salt and pepper.
- Melted butter, cheese, cream, chopped prosciutto.
- Melted butter with some lightly sautéed fresh sage leaves.

Patrick: I am going to throw a monkey wrench into "Mr. Sauce's" category and mention plain old American style gravies. Typical gravies are made from the drippings from the meat that was cooked. Remove most fat and deglaze the pan with wine. To this you add your broth and herbs and/or spices. You then thicken this with a mixture of cold water and flour to the consistency of your liking. Put through a sieve into a serving bowl. That's pretty much it, very simple and plenty of room for improvisation. Ok, now back to "Mr. International"......

John: It's appropriate that he would throw a "monkey" wrench into it! Actually, the way to make a good "drippings" gravy is to remove most of the fat, stir in flour a wooden spoonful at a time until you have a nice non-greasy paste, then over heat start adding water a little at a time, cooking and stirring it until you've reached your desired consistency. If the meat was well seasoned to begin with, you don't have to add spices. And you don't have to strain your gravy, because the little burned-on pieces of meat that you scrape up when you add the flour are a great flavoring. Patrick just is a little anal at times.

Patrick: Fine, don't strain the gravy, but the little pieces of whatever may be in there have already imparted their flavor so you don't need to bite into the actual "thing". I will be straining my gravy to avoid hard, unneeded "debris". John's wife has used the Heimlich maneuver a number of times on him because he refuses to strain. Case closed!

Polenta

I like polenta. A lot of people don't. But you're missing something if you don't include it in you repertoire of "pasta" dishes. Typically the polenta is cooked for almost an hour before it's done, then poured onto a platter, or a large wood cutting board, and the sauce is poured over it. It is not mixed together, and each diner takes some polenta and some of the sauce on top of it with a large serving spoon.

Patrick: This is funny because polenta is one of the true peasant dishes that just doesn't seem to make the cut with the chic food cliques.

John: Right! You rarely if ever see it as a "mush" with sauce poured over it. But you see it sometimes as a grilled square of cooked, cooled polenta. Usually as a little "decoration" next to the main course on the plate. It adds "chi-chi" value at fancy restaurants. Having said that though, I often make polenta in the summer.

- I cool it in a layer in an oiled baking dish, cut it into squares, brush it with oil, and grill it over charcoal.
- I like to make a porcini mushroom ragu for polenta, by using something like the Bolognese sauce, but omitting the meat, adding more soaked mushrooms and their liquor, and cooking for less time.
- And although Pat would object to the "hi-falootin-ness" of this idea, if you can find fresh mascarpone and truffles anywhere close by, dollop some of the fresh cheese on each serving of fresh hot polenta, and shave some truffle on each. That's as simple and decadent as I get, folks. (This is offered at "Zuni Café" in San Francisco, my other favorite Tuscan restaurant in the States).

To cook polenta

- Boil well-salted water (4 cups of water to one cup of polenta meal).
- Polenta is just plain old ground corn. I use a medium - course grind, not too fine.
- Whisking constantly, pour the polenta in a fine stream into the boiling water. Keep whisking until you're sure there are no lumps and the mush is consistent.
- Switching to a wooden spoon, keep stirring until it thickens.
- Turn the flame down to very, very low and cover the pot tightly.
- Every now and then stir the polenta briskly, so it doesn't stick, and begin "stretching" it into an almost "elastic" consistency.
- If it's not done, but getting too, too thick, add a little boiling water and keep cooking and stirring. Polenta that is not done will taste a little raw and corn-mealy.

Pesto (with interruptions by "The Pesto Pest")

John: I'm pretty sure pesto sauce doesn't literally mean "basil, oil, pignoli, parmigiano, and garlic", but that's the more or less classic recipe.

Patrick: Pesto in its purest form is oil, basil and garlic. Improvisation is accepted.

John: So that's a good start. But be sure to use fresh basil, grate your own good parmigiano, and use a good olive oil.

Patrick: Ok, I gotta say this and I don't give a crap if anybody agrees with me. There is a cheese from Lombardia called Grana Padano. It is a grana as is the Reggiano parmigiano but to me the Padano is better!. It is sharper in taste and it is my preference, though not widely available. I hear people say over and over "Reggiano, Reggiano, blah, blah, blah ..." It is good, I use it, but not my first choice. Capice?

John: Put everything, except the oil, in a food processor, and grind it up. Or you can grind it all with a mortar and pestle, but why bother?. Add the oil slowly through the feed tube until you've got the consistency you want. Salt and pepper as you see fit. I eat pesto rarely, mainly because it's so damn heavy. And typically I reserve it for use on fresh potato gnocchi that I make myself. (See Gnocchi recipe page 87).
But pesto can also be other green herbs, and other kinds of nuts. Walnuts are often used instead of pignoli. Or try a mixture of fresh mint, parsley, and basil, with butter, cream, and cheese over some fresh egg noodles.
A lighter pesto – leave out the nuts and cheese.

Patrick: An even lighter pesto - 3 tbsp of chopped fresh basil and 1 cup air. Serve with a big bowl of steam. You'll love it!

John: And that's why there's a "pest" in pesto, folks!

Purees, Broths, and Reductions

John: Much of this is by way of demonstrating the art of "Not Wasting Things". For example:

> 🍽 *During tomato season when they start piling up on your table and you can't slice and eat them fast enough with just a little salt, pepper, olive oil and some fresh basil, cut each tomato in half and throw them into a large stock pot. Fill it right up to the top, put it over low heat, but add no water. Simmer, and stir occasionally until it's all a big tomato slurry. Add a bunch of salt and reduce so it's a little thickish. Let cool a little and put through a food mill. Freeze this puree in yogurt containers to use in the dead of Winter.*

It tastes fresh from the garden when you're making tomato-based sauces. You can also make this puree in-season for the base of many sauces.

Patrick: That's just wonderful, man, if you have a huge bounty of tomatoes from a large garden, or farmers on every corner. But for the rest of planet, store-bought tomatoes, in or out of season, or good grade canned are fine and will suffice. I guess my job here in this book is to tell you don't stress about not having the best and freshest, but dealing with what you have around.

John: I'm glad we've finally figured out what Pat's role is here. Of course I agree, that you use what you can find available. But what I'm also trying to stress is that good food starts with good ingredients. The recipe can be no better than what you start with. For example, using a store hybrid tomato that you buy in January could be fine cooked down into a sauce with herbs and spices, but would never, ever suffice sliced as a salad with a good fresh mozzarella, oil, and fresh basil. That would be an abomination. So, the rule here has to be, if you can't get the right ingredients for a specific recipe, don't make it.

Patrick: I hope he starts talking about reductions soon, like reducing his blabber on what is politically correct in the kitchen and avoiding that dreadful faux pas of an incorrect tomato.

Fresh Tomato Puree Sauces

- Put some olive oil in a saucepan.
- Add some basil and chopped garlic.
- Sautee lightly for a few seconds.
- Add some tomato puree and simmer a while.
- Salt and Pepper.
    -or-
- Sautee garlic and hot pepper flakes in some oil.
- Add tomato puree and simmer.
- Add vodka and simmer.
- Add cream and simmer.
- Salt and pepper and parsley garnish.
    -or-

- Simmer tomato puree with butter and a whole peeled onion.
- Salt and pepper.

  -or-
- Throw a piece of Parmigiano rind into a tomato sauce while it's cooking, for extra "who's to know" richness.

Broths

When you wind up with fresh or roasted chicken carcasses, beef bones and trimmings, or fresh seafood trimmings, keep them in a plastic bag in the freezer until you have enough to make a batch of broth. Similarly, keep carrot, onion, garlic, celery, and parsley peelings in the freezer.

Patrick: If you are having people over you really don't care for, I usually substitute chicken, etc. with road kill. Use the skins to make Daniel Boone hats to create a fun "frontier" theme. As always, decline giving away the recipe by saying it's a chef's secret.

John: Ignore that man behind the curtain.

- Throw the frozen chicken carcass into a pot of water with some of the odori trimmings and simmer for several hours. Cool, strain, and freeze in yogurt containers. Oh! Did I forget to tell you to eat lots of good yogurt with all the live, active organisms? It's good for you and gives you lots of freezing containers.
- Roast beef bones in the oven for a while and throw out the excess grease. Put the bones into a pot with water and vegetable trimming, boil , strain, and freeze.
- Boil shrimp shells, fish trimmings after filleting the whole fish, with some light odori, strain and freeze.

These are all great when you're making soups, braising meats, or making risotto.
Here's an interesting sauce you can make out of shrimp shells, for example.

A Provençal Shrimp Flavored Sauce

I've taken liberty with Erick Vedel's version of this sauce to be used with fried shrimp balls (made with shrimp and pork), because he is a true chef and I don't have the patience to adhere to his level of detail.

INGREDIENTS: Fresh shrimp in their shells (with heads if available), shallot, tomato puree, olive oil, hazelnuts, almonds.

- Sautee shrimp shells in oil, drain, and simmer in water.
- Sautee shallot in olive oil.
- Add tomato puree and simmer.
- Add shrimp broth and simmer.
- Add very finely ground hazelnuts and almonds.

Obviously the types of sauces, the kinds of pasta, and their combinations are countless. Your mission, should you decide to accept it, is to find your own favorite, personal combinations.

Some other basic, basic, basic sauces

John: *Balsamella (or béchamel, or "basic white sauce")*

INGREDIENTS: Butter, flour, salt and pepper, nutmeg, milk.

- Melt butter in a saucepan.
- Stir in some flour to make a cooked paste.
- Add some salt and pepper, and if you want some nutmeg.
- Which in heated milk.
- Stir until thickened.
- Cool in another bowl with a covering on plastic wrap (if you're not going to use right away).

The proportions of butter, flour, and milk can be varied depending on what recipe you're going to use the sauce in (e.g. lasagna, creamed vegetables, etc.). A typical combination is:

- Four tablespoons of butter
- ¼ cup of flour
- 1-2 cups of milk depending on desired consistency.

Patrick: The cooked paste he is referring to has a name. It's called a "roux". You should simmer the roux to cook the flour before adding your liquid.

John: My dog would say, "arooooo…!" when howling at the moon. In Creole cooking, which tends to be more popular these days in America, than French cooking, the roux has lost the butter component (in the Cajun version) and replaced it with oil or melted lard. For instance in our mother's "Shrimp Creole" which she picked up in Mobile, the flour is stirred into oil. In the typical Cajun roux a lot of fat is used and the flour is browned very slowly for a very long time, so that the flour is very well cooked and takes on a rich deep brown color. But not burned! This is the basis of any Creole gumbo or jambalaya.

Aioli, etc.

Also referred to often as "maionnese" in Italian cookbooks. This is also inspired by Erick's use of fresh lemon juice and Dijon mustard in his aioli.

INGREDIENTS: Garlic, salt, lemon juice (not from a phony plastic lemon), Dijon mustard, olive oil.

- Puree some garlic in a dish with some salt and lemon juice.
- Place an egg yolk into a heavy, smallish bowl.
- Add a little Dijon mustard and some salt.
- While slowing dripping a half cup of olive oil into the bowl, whish the mixture continually,

and with verve, until all the oil is gone and the mixture is stiff and smooth.

• Beat in the garlic.

To spice this up and call it "Rouille" (roo-eee), a Provençal rendition used with soups:

• Beat in a little paprika and some cayenne powder.
• Add an egg yolk before beating in olive oil.

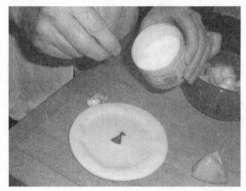
A pinch of salt in the lemon juice

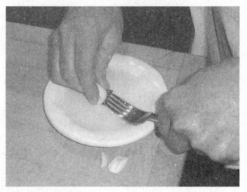
Pureeing garlic clove on fork tines

Whisk in olive oil

Reductions

John: This is as simple as:

• Boiling down braising liquids to form a sauce. These may be strained or not.
  -or-
• De-glazing a pan in which vegetables, fish, or meats have been seared or sautéed by pouring some sweet red or dry white vermouth into the hot skillet while stirring and scraping up stuck-on food bits and fat until a thickish, smooth sauce is formed.
  -or-
• Simmering down broths to a very rich base.

Reductions take on a more naturally thick consistency if you start with something that has some marrow in it, like shanks, ox tails, pig's foot, etc.. There! Sauces have been de-mystified. They're all simple. If you want to get exotic, buy an exotic French cookbook (like La Bonne Cuisine, by Madame E. Saint-Ange). I'm sure the results will be exquisite.

Patrick: Can't you just picture him in the kitchen dressed nice with a light cardigan and bow tie, or possibly a frilly apron and heels?

John: No, our intelligent readers can't picture that because I don't cook from exotic French cookbooks. Even Julia Child eschewed strict protocol. He is such wise guy. It's a good thing he lives on the other coast!

Patrick: I'll say it's a good thing I live so far away. He might have thrown a napkin at me!

Pasta

John: If you make a dish in which fresh pasta is required, you should consider making your own. If you don't need pasta, buy something imported from Italy. In Italy, each of the many regions has its own shapes and names of dried pasta. Dried pasta is usually just a hard wheat flour and water. Of course in each region they make different kinds of pasta sauces. Consequently you might pick up an eclectic recipe book on Italian cooking or find something in a magazine that looks good to you. Usually it specifies the particular shape and size of dried pasta to make for the particular sauce in the recipe. There are arguments that certain types of sauces go best with certain shapes of pasta. For example if the sauce is say a thin, non-chunky style, it might be best to serve with a pasta that has a curves or ridges that help hold the sauce. And vice versa for thicker, chunkier sauces. That's all well and good, but if I were you I'd find my own favorite dried pastas, and my own favorite sauce recipes, and figure out what you like best and what works for you. Most cooking is not autocratic and not written in stone. As Patrick would say (and he stole this from an old proverb) "the cooking is in the hand of the cook". That's you!

Patrick: Again, he listens with his mouth open. The saying is, *"the secret is in ......"*. Since John is bringing up that cooking is not "autocratic", maybe now is a good time to bring up a point. Typically, in my opinion, recipes that are very old, time tested, and have proven themselves to be of the very best and authentic are figuratively written in stone. Therefore if you are to make them, then you should follow the recipes to the letter. That is not to say you can't alter them later on. I am just saying that if you like the "looks" of a recipe you see, make it exactly as described before altering. Basically, what you are doing here is experiencing the original form, and then you ask yourself, "Do I like it enough to stick to it, or would I like it with a little twist on something here or there?"

John: I stand corrected. Though I've never seen Patrick follow any recipe exactly, so I'm wondering what he's *talkin'* about. But for now we'll focus on making fresh pasta, and recipes that use it. OK here's one of my infernal "notes".

The cuisines that predominate in Western culture are obviously French and Italian. They are very different in many ways in their treatments of meats, vegetables, rice, sauces, and most other food genres (except for Provençal cuisine, which is very Italian). The thing that really separates French from Italian though is that the French don't have the whole genre of pasta. Sure, you may find some pasta things in France, but they're after-thoughts, side dishes, a little starch to balance the meal. Starches in France are typically potatoes, and they do potatoes very, very well. In some places, rice is a main starch. In Italy, pasta is genre of food that not only stands on its own, as its own course, but is, dare I say, the soul of Italian cuisine. Likewise in France one may well successfully argue that wine is the centerpiece of French cuisine, and that recipes are essentially created to enhance wine. While in Italy the wine is the supporting cast member to the food, the star. Therefore the pasta itself is the center of Italian cooking, not the sauce that goes on it, or the meat it goes with, or the stuffing inside the ravioli. The sauce, or the stuffing, supports the pasta. The pasta is the first star listed on the marquee. Whether Marco Polo brought noodles back from China, or whether the Etruscans invented it as wheat gruel in ancient Tuscany, doesn't matter at this point.

Patrick: I love pasta no matter where it hails from, and *if* I go out to eat, and *if* it's an ethnic restaurant, I will usually order some kind of pasta. At home it's normal for our family to eat Italian, American and Slovak (my wife's heritage) dishes that have some version of pasta in them. Obviously, pasta, macaroni, noodles or whatever you want to call this form of food, made with water, flour, and maybe egg is a staple in many places all over the galaxy.

John: So that's where Patrick was tripping off to, when he should have been studying in college! Wonder what the name of said galaxy was – "Lucy In The Sky With Diamonds"?

"Basic" Fresh Pasta

Typically the recipe for fresh pasta is roughly one cup of all purpose, unbleached white flour, to one large egg, plus maybe a drizzle of olive oil and some salt. Pasta in the old days, and in some places still, was made by rolling the dough out on a large table. I strongly urge you to buy a good quality, heavy duty Italian made hand-cranked pasta rolling machine, as Patrick has already recommended.

INGREDIENTS: All-purpose white unbleached flour, olive oil, eggs, salt.

* Measure out the flour in a mountain shape onto work surface.
* With the bottom of your measuring cup, make a crater in the mountain large enough to handle the eggs.
* Add some salt and olive oil to the eggs.
* Carefully begin beating the eggs with a fork. Don't let the crater overflow.
* Gradually incorporate flour into the eggs a little a time with the fork from the inside edge of the crater.
* When the egg/flour mixture gets stiff enough, pick it up and shape it into a large ball.
* Put the unused flour though a sifter to remove small chunks of dough. Toss them out.
* Begin kneading the dough with your hands, incorporating a little flour at a time until you have a smooth, not sticky, but not too dense or too dry a ball of yellowish dough.
* Divide the large ball into pieces that are about the size of a baseball.
* Roll them in a little flour and put them into a plastic bag to rest and to keep them from drying out while you set up your rolling machine.
* Taking one ball of dough at a time, put it through the thickest setting of the machine. Each time flour the flat piece lightly and fold it into thirds. Flatten it a little at one edge with your palm against the table, and put it through the same wide setting again. Add a little flour each time if the dough gets too sticky.
* Repeat this on the widest setting several times until the dough is no longer sticky and is very smooth and elastic.
* Then, without folding the dough into thirds, crank the roller setting up one notch to the next thinnest setting and put the dough through, once per setting.
* Keep cranking it up until you're at about # 6 or #7 setting (about 1/16, of an inch roughly). Each time you'll have a longer and longer sheet. Kids love to stand in a line along the kitchen floor and drape the sheet across their hands, and help you feed it back into the next setting on the machine. A friend of mine once asked me if this was sanitary. I reminded him that at some point the pasta was to be boiled.

Crack eggs into flour crater

Beat eggs, salt, and oil

Work wet dough into a mass with scraper

Separate dough into balls

Start to stretch each ball

Fold dough into thirds

Final stretch

At this point, it depends what you're going to make with the pasta before you go ahead and roll the next ball out. If for example you want to make lasagna, cut each sheet into pieces about 6 inches long, and lay them on dish towels, not overlapping, somewhere. Roll out all the balls of dough one at a time, cut them, and lay them out on the towels too. Too make noodles, cut the pieces longer, and lay them out to dry a little. It makes them easier to cut so the noodles separate into individual strands more cleanly without sticking.

For stuffed pastas, take each sheet as you finish rolling it out and make your ravioli, etc. before you go to the next ball of dough.

Flavored and Colored Fresh Pastas

It is very acceptable, and traditional, to color and flavor your fresh pasta:

Green pasta: Replace some of the egg with some cooked and finely chopped or pureed spinach (but make sure you blanch and quickly cool the fresh spinach properly first to retain its bright green color – see the vegetable section)

Chop cooked and drained spinach

Mix chopped spinach into eggs

Red pasta: Replace some of the egg with cooked, peeled, and finely chopped (or pureed) beets. Or use tomato paste. Or roasted, pureed peppers.

Bright yellow: Add some finely crushed saffron to the eggs.

Herbal: You can "em-bed" some whole fresh leaves of parsley, basil, etc. in between sheets of pasta and run the "herb sandwich" through the finest roller setting one last time.

Spicy: Add some pepper, or other ground spices to the egg.

For example, the spinach pasta works well with a meatless lasagna. The beet pasta might work well as a ravioli with a complementary filling (say a goat cheese). The saffron with a fish stuffing. And so on. (Actually, I just made this up. But they might work out fine.)

Patrick: The reason you want a hand-cranked pasta machine, or for that matter any hand operated kitchen utensil, is that it brings you closer to the food, allowing you to get to know it and become one with it, so to speak. Same as in sports for example. You need to be in "the zone" in order to perform well. You *must* buy the best quality you can afford. John speaks of letting the pasta sheet dry a little so it separates better when cutting strips. First of all, the dough should not be that "wet" for that to occur, and secondly, if it happens too often you probably need a new machine. I had a machine that had an issue with strips not cutting cleanly, so I replaced it with a better machine and presto! The problem disappeared. There will be times if you are feeling especially energetic that rolling out the dough by hand on a board will be necessary if you are making a stuffed pasta roll for example. Unless you have a commercial wide machine, there is no other way to do it. Either way, if for no other reason, try rolling it out by hand just for the experience. It is grunt work, and it teaches you patience and dedication. One more quick note: if the filling you are using for any stuffed pasta is overly wet it will destroy the pasta and turn it into a gloppy mess. Excess liquid from ricotta, or any filling, should be drained or squeezed out first, and the bottom and tops or the finished ravioli should be lightly floured to help "preserve" them before cooking, which, unless you freeze them, should be done shortly after assembling them.

John: I always like to make a thin paste of flour and water to help seal the ravioli top and bottom together.

Again, I can't emphasize enough using the best quality flour and the best quality eggs. You'll see what I mean if you experiment with different qualities of each ingredient.

Patrick: Yeah, yeah, yeah. Enough already. We get the idea that fresh is best, now let it go. Everybody understands that by now, hopefully.

Well, you're now entitled to see the correct way of making fresh pasta. My corrections are in *italics*.

- Measure out the flour in a mountain shape onto *large* work surface.
- With *your fingers extended and their tips touching, start at the center of the mound and in circular motions create a well, essentially a crater with walls on the edges. The well you create should be about 6-8 inches in diameter and the walls about ½"-1" high.*
- Add a *pinch* of salt and *very small drizzle of* olive oil *and the egg.*
- Carefully begin beating the eggs with a fork. Don't let the crater overflow.
- Gradually incorporate flour into the eggs a little a time with the fork from the inside edge of the crater.
- When the egg/flour mixture *begins to form a rough mass, start using a stainless steel pastry scraper to help in adding more flour and bringing the edges over in a folding, almost preliminary kneading style. When it just gets to the point where you can handle the lump of dough, pick it up and set it aside.*
- Put the unused flour though a sifter to remove small chunks of dough. Toss them out.
- *Return your dough to the surface with the cleaned flour,* and begin kneading the dough with your hands, incorporating a little flour at a time until you have a smooth, not sticky, but not too dense or dry ball of yellowish dough.
- Divide the ball into *2 equal size pieces.*
- Roll them in a little flour and put them into a plastic bag to rest and to keep them from drying out while you set up your rolling machine.
- Taking one ball of dough at a time, *flatten out by hand on a floured surface and then* put it through the thickest setting of the machine. Each time flour the flat piece lightly and fold it into thirds. Flatten it a little at one edge with your palm against the table, and put it through the same wide setting again.

- Repeat this on the widest setting several times until the dough is no longer sticky and is very smooth and elastic.
- Then, without folding the dough into thirds, crank the roller setting up one notch to the next thinnest setting and put the dough through.
- *Continue this process, lightly flouring both sides* until you're at about # 6 or #7 setting (about 1/16, or slightly more, of an inch roughly). Each time you'll have a longer and longer sheet. I love to stand in a line along the kitchen floor and drape the sheet across their hands, and help you feed it back into the next setting on the machine. *Sorry, I am not into the guests and kids swarming around the kitchen getting in the way of serious business.*

John: Patrick is not that serious, but truly is a wise-ass at heart, who happens to also like kids. I'm not offended, by the way, that Patrick has his own obscure way of making his dough. Make pasta either way, and it'll turn out great once you've practiced enough. In fact, you'll probably wind up concocting your own idiosyncratic method. Which is the point of this book, after all. Following are some of my versions of some staple fresh pasta based recipes:

A Spinach and Ricotta Ravioli – a basic stuffed pasta

A Typical Stuffing

Almost any stuffing should:
- Include some egg and some grated parmigiano cheese for flavoring and binding.
- Should not be wet or runny.
- Should not be too chunky, or the chunks could puncture the thin pasta.

INGREDIENTS: Fresh pasta sheets, fresh or frozen spinach, ricotta, egg, parmigiano, nutmeg.

- For this dish, use either fresh or frozen spinach. After cooking, chop very finely and squeeze all the moisture out in a cotton towel. Put the spinach in a large bowl.
- Dump the container of ricotta into some cheesecloth or towel, and it squeeze it out, too, and add it to the bowl.
- Crack an egg into the bowl.
- Grate some parmigiano into the bowl.
- Salt. Italians, especially Tuscans, are not afraid of using sufficient salt in their recipes.
- Freshly grated nutmeg.
- Maybe a little pepper.
- Mix well with a wooden spoon.

At this point you're ready to stuff. I use a ravioli frame about 5 inches wide and about 12 inches long that you can find in any kitchen supply store. I don't like to use the stuffing attachments that you can get with the rolling machine. Or you can just lay out a sheet of pasta on a lightly floured surface, made teaspoon-sized dollops of filling, spaced far enough apart to make ravioli about 2"-3" square (or round) each.

- Either way, trace out the squares on the sheet between the dollops with your finger lightly moistened in some floury water as a glue.
- Then lay another slightly larger sheet on top and press down around the dollops to seal.
- Cut with a pastry wheel, then crimp the ravioli around the edges with fork.
- Lay the ravioli (ravioli, not raviolis, is the plural of ravioli)on a cotton dish towel.
- When all the ravioli are made, simmer them, in salted water. Fresh pasta takes only a minute or so to cook. Fresh cooked noodles or ravioli will float to the surface when done. Drain them well in a colander in the sink, or drain on towels.

I like to use some melted butter in which some fresh sage leaves have been lightly, lightly, lightly sautéed as the sauce. Grind some fresh pepper on top.

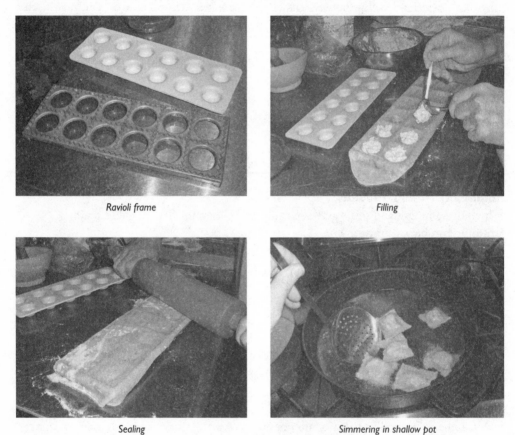

Ravioli frame

Filling

Sealing

Simmering in shallow pot

Squash Filling

INGREDIENTS: A winter squash, egg, breadcrumbs, nutmeg.

- Stick a whole squash in a hot oven and roast until done, testing with a wood skewer.
- Remove from oven, cool, peel, clean out the seeds and stringy pulp, and puree.
- Add some egg, unseasoned breadcrumbs, salt and pepper, and maybe a little fresh ground nutmeg.
- Sauce could be melted butter and fresh grated parmigiano (see page 60).

A Meat Stuffing

INGREDIENTS: Braised meat, or sausage meat removed from casings, egg, parmigiano, breadcrumbs. See the **"Braising"** lesson (page 105) for techniques for cooking meat for meat fillings.

- You could take the meat from braising beef shanks, chop it up, add some egg, parmigiano, and breadcrumbs.
- Or cut the casing away from some good fresh sweet Italian sausage (with no fennel), and sauté the meat until it's no longer pink, de-grease, cool, and add some egg, etc.
- Or anything else you might invent. Genoese fishermen went to sea for extended periods with some meat and vegetables for a diet, using any scraps and leftovers for ravioli fillings. So the whole point of stuffed pastas is making up recipes with whatever you have.
- Chop up the meat and whatever vegetables you braised it in, mix with breadcrumbs, parmigiano, eggs.

Good with a tomato-based meat sauce, like a good Bolognese.

Lasagne

John: This where fresh pasta gets really, really good. Here are a couple of ideas to work from.

Patrick: A little side note before John continues with his lasagna recipes. Technically, a lasagna would have at least 14 layers of pasta, essentially an Italian term describing buildings with many floors. On the other hand you also have what is called a "ripiena" which is a stuffed pasta or layered pasta consisting of only a few layers.

Cut into squares

Cook pasta sheets

Cool cooked pasta sheets in cold water

Cooked pasta sheets resting

A layer of pasta sheets overlapping edge

Sauce layer

Ricotta or Balsamella layer

Mozzarella layer

Final assembly

Lasagna Al Forno

INGREDIENTS: Lean meat (chicken, pork, veal beef), ingredients to braise the meat (see the Braising lesson page 105), balsamella (see page 65), fresh mozzarella, parmigiano, fresh pasta cut into 6 inch lengths,

- Make a meat filling (e.g. chop up a cheap cut of lean meat into very fine chunks, and then braise it) cooking for a long time, covered on top of the stove. You don't want a dry sauce, but not soupy either. The well-cooked meat with fall apart into very small shreds.
- Make a balsamella (see page 65).
- Grate some fresh mozzarella into a bowl, and mix into it some fresh ground parmigiano.
- Make fresh pasta, cutting it into lengths about 6 inches long.
- Boil the pasta sheets briefly until they float, a few at a time, in salted water.
- Using tongs, put the boiled pasta into cold water that has a little oil in it.
- Lay the cooked sheets, in a single layer, not overlapping, on dry cotton towels.

Assemble the lasagna:
- Spread a light layer of sauce on the bottom of a glass or ceramic baking dish.
- Put one layer of pasta on the bottom allowing the pasta to drape over the edge of the dish.
- Fill in the bottom of the dish with more sheets to cover the sauce in one layer only.
- Cover the pasta with sauce.
- Put another layer of pasta sheet over the sauce. Only cover the bottom of the dish, don't let the subsequent layers of pasta drape over the edge of the dish.
- Sprinkle a layer of the cheese mixture on the pasta.
- Add another layer of pasta.
- Spread a layer of the balsamella.
- Another layer of pasta.
- More sauce.
- Continue layering until the dish is filled up and/or the ingredients are gone, but saving a little sauce for the top.
- Flop the edges of the bottom layer of pasta over the top to form a nice pasta "package".
- Spread the remaining sauce over the top.
- Bake the lasagna in a medium/hot oven for about a half hour or so.
- Let sit at room temperature to set, then cut into large squares to serve.

A Vegetarian Style
(Not necessarily just for vegetarians)

INGREDIENTS: Fresh pasta using fresh or frozen spinach (cooked and chopped in place of some of the eggs), garlic, olive oil, tomato puree, ricotta, mozzarella, parmigiano, nutmeg, fresh basil leaves.

- Make fresh pasta, but use some cooked, finely chopped spinach instead of some of the eggs when making the dough. Roll and pre-cook the pasta sheets as above.
- Make a light sauce by sautéing some garlic in a little olive oil, then adding some good tomato puree from a box or can and simmering a little while.
- Make a stuffing by mixing ricotta, softened butter, parmigiano, salt, pepper, and nutmeg.
- Grate some good mozzarella into another bowl and mix with some salt and pepper.
- Assemble the lasagna in alternating ingredient layers as above. Spread the fresh basil leaves in the sauce layers.
- Bake and serve as above.

Patrick: I have repeatedly told my wife to not buy any meat aside from chicken, but she still attempts to do so because the price looked good and she was in the mood for a steak on the grill. Well, just recently this happened again. She bought this "steak" that must have cost 10 cents a pound by the looks of it. She actually bought two and she grilled one and admitted it was not like a Porterhouse! Anyway, a week or so later she took the other out of the freezer leaving it up to me to do something with it. So here is a recipe that I just made up and the end result...... Wow! Now this may be a little demanding on you as far as the pasta goes unless you have some pasta making experience. The pasta must be rolled out by hand with a rolling pin into one thin sheet.

Rotolo di Bistecca Bruto Ripieno
(Stuffed ugly steak roll)

THE STUFFING INGREDIENTS: Some king of cheap ugly, bone in "steak". Remove as much fat as possible and cut the meat parts into chunks. Celery coarsely chopped, carrots peeled and coarsely chopped, onion thinly sliced, bay leaves, fresh chopped parsley, chicken broth, red wine, some olive oil, whole cloves garlic, a few stalks asparagus, tomato paste, salt & pepper, provolone cheese thinly sliced.

THE PASTA INGREDIENTS: Flour, eggs, some salt, some olive oil.

THE BALSAMELLA INGREDIENTS: Butter, garlic oil, flour, milk, nutmeg.

For the meat filling:
- Braise meat with the odori, wine, and broth (see Braising lesson page 105).
- Then remove the top and let the liquid begin to reduce. The meat should be pretty tender at this point.
- Remove the meat with a slotted spoon and set aside in a bowl to cool.
- Add the asparagus to the broth and simmer.
- In the mean time, remove and chop up the meat, remove any bones and fat.
- Throw the meat into a bowl with any of the vegetables that got in your slotted spoon.
- Remove the asparagus from the broth and cut into pieces and add to the meat mixture.
- Add the tomato paste and stir together. Add all this back into the broth.
- Let reduce under very thick then set aside to cool.

For the pasta:
- Follow the general procedure of creating the ball of dough (see page 71). Let rest a couple of minutes.
- Flour your pastry board.
- Flatten out the dough and begin rolling out with your rolling pin.
- To flip the dough, roll the pasta on the pin then unroll it onto its other side back onto the board which you have again floured.
- Keep up with this process until you have achieved and then rectangular sheet.
- Let the dough rest.
- Boil salted water in a very large pot.
- Add the sheet of pasta being careful not to let it fold up. The cooking should only take about 30 seconds.
- Remove to a large bowl of cold water then spread out onto a clean dry towel.

Putting together the roll:
- Place the provolone on the sheet of pasta but do not over lap.
- Spoon the meat filling over the cheese and spread evenly throughout.
- Begin rolling the pasta from the short end. It may help to lift the towel and let the roll form by just falling away from the towel as to lift and curl it over, sort of.
- When the roll has been formed place in an oiled baking dish.

FOR THE BALSAMELLA:
- Make balsamella (see page 65).
- Spoon some of this over the top of the roll.
- Add more milk to the remaining sauce until it is thinner and gravy like.
- Take off heat and cover.

Place the roll in a preheated medium oven until it begins to golden. Remove from oven to rack and cool on rack.

To serve, slice into thick pieces and put onto plates on their sides revealing the cross section. Spoon some of balsamella over each serving. You're done and you can eat now.

Fresh Tagliatelli with Prosciutto, Cream, and Gorgonzola Sauce

INGREDIENTS: Fresh saffron pasta sheets, heavy cream, butter, gorgonzola cheese, prosciutto, pepper.

- Cut fresh pasta into "spaghetti" lengths, and cut these into widths of about a quarter inch. Most pasta rolling machines will have a cutter with this width.
- Sauté some chopped prosciutto in butter.
- Add cream and crumbled gorgonzola, and heat through to simmer , and until the cheese melts slightly.

Serve with plenty of fresh pepper.

Gnocchi

Made right, the gnocchi should be very light and "fluffy". Combined with just a slight coating of the heavy pesto, it's a nice balance. To make your own gnocchi:

- Combine mashed or riced cooked potato, flour, and egg - like you're making fresh pasta.
- Roll out the dough into snake-like lengths and cut it into one inch pieces.
- Shape them into a sort of "C" with the tines of a fork. This gives the gnocchi some ridges to hold the pesto better.
- Boil until they float.
- Drain well.

Practice, practice, practice makes lighter, lighter, lighter gnocchi. Experiment with different types of potatoes. I think baking potatoes are best because they're "floury" when cooked.

Put cooked potato through food mill

Roll balls of dough into ropes

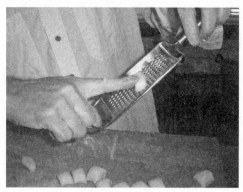
Forming Gnocchi on cheese grater

Finished Gnocchi

Bocconcini di Parma

Technically not pasta, but crepes. But where else would I stick a recipe that is a real exquisite treat?

INGREDIENTS: Butter, flour, eggs, milk, salt, nutmeg, pepper (Pat would prefer white pepper), ricotta, parmigiano.

Prepare the stuffing:
• Drain a container of ricotta and stir in a few eggs, grated Parmigiano, some soft butter (about half a stick), some pepper, and some nutmeg.
• I always like to freshly grate whole nutmegs when I use it for flavoring.
• Mix well.

Prepare the crepes:
Crepe proportions are a TB of butter, to a cup of flour, a cup of milk, 2 eggs.
• Melt and cool butter.
• Make a batter of the cooled butter, flour, eggs, a cup of milk, and some salt, pepper, and nutmeg. The batter should be a little thin to make a nice thin crepe.
• Cover bowl and let rest in refrigerator for an hour.
• Buttering in between each crepe as you make them, spread the batter evenly on a hot griddle to about the size of a corn tortilla. Stack the finished crepes separately between waxed paper.

Assemble and bake the crespelle:
• Put some filling on each crepe, and roll up. Put them in the refrigerator to rest.
• Cut them into shorter rolls a couple of inches long.
• Place them on end in a heavily buttered baking dish.
• Bake in a medium/hot until they start to brown on top.

Savory Tarts

Savory tarts, at least in the Tuscan tradition, or probably any tradition, are essentially a baked one crust pie with a filling concoction.

Tart shells

See the Dessert lesson (page 164) for a basic crust. Partially bake the crust with weights. Use a fluted edge tart pan if you have one, with a removable bottom.

Fillings

Wild Mushroom

INGREDIENTS: Dried porcini or other dried wild (non-toxic and non-hallucinogenic) 'shrooms, onion, parsley, olive oil, butter, tomato paste, beef broth, eggs, parmigiano.

- Soak, drain, and chop the porcini after they're softened.
- Saute chopped onion and parsley in olive oil and butter.
- Add chopped mushrooms to pan and sauté.
- Add tomato paste, stir, and sauté.
- Add broth (with some of the mushroom soaking liquid) and salt and pepper.
- Cook until thick.
- Let cool.
- Mix in beaten egg and parmigiano.

Others to try

All of these will use eggs as binders, maybe some bread crumbs (if you wish) and some broth of some kind (if necessary). Also usually some parmigiano, and sometimes some heavy cream – depending.

- *Tomato:* Make a thick tomato sauce with tomato puree and odori. Let cool completely before mixing with eggs, etc. Flavor with some basil.

- *Spinach:* I'll use either fresh or frozen spinach, but make sure it's not over-cooked so it doesn't lose its bright green color. Squeeze all the liquid out – I mean all! Flavor with some fresh ground nutmeg, and add some ricotta (again, well drained).

- *Squash and rice:* Bake and puree the winter squash. Blend with cooked Arborio rice. Add lots of parmigiano. Try nutmeg, too.

- *Seafood:* Use white fish and small shrimp, and try flavoring with bay, garlic, and a little hot pepper.

- *Potato and Leek:* Boil and rice potatoes. Sautee leeks in oil and chopped pancetta. Flavor with fresh rosemary.

John: Yes, fresh pastas can be time-consuming, but it goes quicker than you think if you have a few tries under your belt. And it's fun thing to do with kids, or with guests, especially if you're sharing some good wine and you just relax about it. (Regardless of what Patrick may say. He just gets a little grumpy every month or so).

Soups and Beans

John: A couple of thoughts to start this lesson. First, I love beans. I also love green beans fresh in the summer, but here I mean the dried kind that you cook for a long time. Second, I love soup.

Every time I make a bean dish, or a soup, or a bean soup I announce to those assembled, "I could live on this." And I usually mean it. The dish almost always works out tasting good – actually great! It feels healthful in your belly. It's satisfying, especially accompanied by bread and salad, and often cheese. It's easy. The problem is, I just about always make up the recipe, based on what I have on hand, or at the very least bastardize one in a cookbook so extremely, that I never remember what I did. Even though my wife will say, "You *have* to remember this one!" Of course I never do. When she cooks a soup from a recipe, and we both love it, she can always re-create it by simply going back to the cookbook it came from. It doesn't work that way with me. But hey! That's the point of this book, isn't it? It's about doing what you think seems right, and hang the recipe. Or using what you're got in the pantry and fridge, instead of adhering exactly to somebody else's idea of what "Pumpkin Soup with Small White Beans and Cuban Spices" is supposed to have in it. So this, after all, will be more or less how I go about cooking beans, soups, and other such concoctions. And you can take it from there. I don't want to hear about it. Actually this is a good time for one of my tiresome "notes".

> 🍽 Cooking soups and bean dishes is a good example of how I decide what to cook on any given day. Typically I look in the fridge, in the garden, in the pantry, and in the local markets to see what's fresh and good-looking. Then, I'll drag a whole lot of cookbooks off my cookbook shelf, plop down on the couch and find recipes that call for the ingredients I happen to have. I'll glance over a half dozen or so, sometimes from completely different cuisines. Then close all the books and put them away. Then, in my own little head, I make up something using the cookbooks as idea generators and catalysts. Sometime I'm very happy with the results (let's say maybe 25% of the time), sometimes I'm like, "I don't think I'll bother with that again, but it's OK" (about 50% of the time), and sometimes I'm very disappointed (the remaining 25% of the time). Though most people who eat my cooking tell me that my batting average is higher in their estimation, I chalk that up to kindness and the fact that although I'm not a perfectionist, I expect better from myself than I often achieve. But that's what drives me.

Patrick: Soups often tend fall into the cold weather cooking category even if they contain no beans, but especially if they do, since the beans tend to make the soup thicker and therefore heartier. Non-soup bean dishes are fair weather selections since they are typically either served cold mixed with tuna, or just sprinkled with olive oil as a salad for example, or as a heated dish mixed with something else like broccolirab, or just cold baked beans for a barbecue cookout.

My decision on what to cook primarily depends on not only what is available but how much time or energy I have left to create it, depending on the day. On those really "unable to cook days", I may just end up making a peanut butter and jelly sandwich. You got a problem with that? Here is another rule for you: not everything you make has to be more difficult or time consuming than a sandwich.

John: I certainly agree with that. Simplicity *is* our motto! Though I make a lot of fresh summer vegetable style soups in the summer. But just to add a little confusion, in the world of Italian cooking there are basically two genres of soup. There are the minestre and the zuppe. I've cooked both, without ever really figuring out what the difference is. I'm sure there is an acceptable definition somewhere. It has something to do with if the "soup" is brothy or thick, has bread "crouton" in it or not, has pasta or beans or rice or potatoes in it or not, and so on. In the grand scheme of things it really doesn't matter, of course, since this book is *not* all about splitting hairs. The bottom line is, soup is essentially a conglomeration of things that are available, depending on the season, and what you've got laying around. And you usually eat it with a spoon.

Patrick: OK, let me help him out here. You have your broths, minestrones and minestre. All these are basically "soups". The broth is just that. The minestrones are more of typical soup consistency, mainly with vegetables and pasta. The minestre are the thickest of the lot. They are mainly the bean and pasta style dishes and can be quite thick. They all vary from region to region, but whatever you make will be what you prefer as far as consistency, for the most part.

John: He almost sounds like he knows what he's talking about.

A Basic Vegetable Soup

John: I almost always start by seeing what kind of frozen stock I have in the freezer, or what good quality purchased stock I have in the larder. If none, use water.

INGREDIENTS: Water or a light chicken or vegetable stock, vegetables of your choice (see below), olive oil, parmigiano.

- Cut, chop, or slice up, as appropriate, some Savoy cabbage, potato, onion, carrot, parsley, chard, tomatoes, kale, green beans, etc.

> 🍽 *This is what is called a "minestrone". Typically in the winter it would have cold weather growing greens like kale, savoy cabbage, potato, dried beans, chard, and maybe some canned tomatoes. A summer minestrone may have fresh tomatoes, fresh green beans, zucchini, onion, and fresh pasta. Sometimes the cooked soup is all pureed, or some of it is pureed, or none of it is pureed. See what I mean about the beauty of soup? It's the most free-form kind of cooking you can do. And a good place to start teaching you how to ignore recipes and follow your intuition.*

- Chop and sauté the odori type vegetables in some olive oil in a heavy covered soup pot.
- Cook the pre-soaked beans in water, salt, and maybe a piece of prosciutto or pancetta, until tender.
- Add the cooked beans and their cooking liquor to the sautéed odori.
- Add the roughly chopped greens, etc. and simmer.
- Grate some parmigiano over each bowlful, and maybe drizzle a little olive oil over that.
- Grate fresh salt and pepper on it.

Sometimes the cooked soup is put through a food mill, or blender, to make a "passato", or puree. You could also add some small type of pasta or rice to the soup, and cook it through until done.

A Winter Squash Soup

INGREDIENTS: A winter squash, butter, oil, prosciutto, beef broth, parmigiano, fresh parsley, basil, or sage.

- Peel and cut up a winter squash into chunks.
- Sautee the chunks in some butter and oil, and some chopped up prosciutto until tender.
- Put the squash through a food mill.
- Add beef broth and stir and heat together. Add more broth to reach your desired consistency.
- Grate some cheese on top, if you want, or sprinkle some chopped parsley or maybe some sage.

> 🍽 I'll add here a note about preparing Winter squashes, because my wife will ultimately insist that I do, and I don't feel like arguing about it. We learned in Provence that it is not necessary to peel a Winter squash before you cook or eat it. I personally feel that this is fine, if for example you're making a casserole out of the chunked up squash. However I feel that peeling is necessary if you want a smooth puree for making some other type of recipe. She may disagree. Whatever the truth is, you will discover it on your own dime.

A Pasta soup

INGREDIENTS: Broth, small fresh or dried pasta, parmigiano, fresh herbs of your choice.

- Simmer some broth.
- Drop some fresh or dried pasta into the broth.
- Cook until done.
- Grate cheese on each bowlful.
- Add some fresh herbs if you want.

Fish Soup

> 🍽 See **Seafood** lesson (pages 123-124) for Provençal and Tuscan versions of this worldwide and cross-cultural culinary staple.

A Chicken Soup

INGREDIENTS: Chicken broth, leftover chicken, your choice of vegetables, herbs of your choice, uncooked rice.

- Simmer some chicken broth.
- Add some chopped or shredded cooked chicken left over from a roasted chicken.
- Add some chopped vegetables.
- Throw in a bundle of thyme, celery leaves, garlic, and bay leaf. Maybe a star anise.
- Simmer until almost done and add some rice to finish cooking.
- Salt and pepper.

Sometimes in soups I'll add some fresh chopped hot chilies if I feel like I need a little warm glow when I eat the soup. Sometimes I'll put a little bowl of hot chili paste on the table and let people swirl a little into their bowl. Maybe I'll have some slices of lemon or lime to squirt into each bowl as a little citrusy thing.

Nancy's Favorite Soup

John: I made this up one night, which is the beauty of soup, and it's now at least a 2-3 times a month basic in our house. If I want to make my wife happy, foodwise, I'll cook this.

INGREDIENTS: Fish, vegetable, or chicken stock, fresh ginger, garlic, hot chili peppers, bok choy (or other greens like kale, savoy cabbage, chard, etc.), fresh, thick Chinese noodles (udon), firm tofu, fish sauce, soy sauce, sesame oil, citrus (optional).

- Simmer some chicken, or seafood, or vegetable broth in a wok (not necessary to use a wok but this is an "Asian" idea).
- Throw in some finely sliced fresh ginger, sliced hot fresh chilies, sliced or chopped garlic and simmer.
- Add some roughly chopped bok choy, or other greens, and simmer.
- Add some *fresh* thick Chinese noodles and simmer.
- Add some tofu cut into large cubes.
- Before serving put in a *little* fish sauce, soy sauce, sesame oil, and maybe a grate of citrus peel.
- Serve in very large soup bowls with chopsticks to pick up and eat the solid ingredients, and a large spoon to finish slurping up the broth.

You could garnish with scallions or sautéed shitakes, for example.

Posole – A Version of the Classic Mexican Corn Soup

Like my "famous" tofu and udon soup recipe, this is neither Tuscan, Provençal, nor American peasant. It's obviously Mexican. But I'll steal from any good culinary heritage to make a point. My wife, who claims to have gone to Mexico once before we met, says that posole can be made with chicken, probably because she doesn't like to eat pork and is trying to convince me that chicken is more authentic. But any recipe I've ever seen has pork. But I usually go with the flow here, because I like the way posole tastes if I use a leftover mesquite-smoked chicken carcass.

INGREDIENTS: Pork shoulder cut into chunks, or a chicken (fresh and cut up, or roasted and the meat pulled off the carcass), canned white corn "hominy" (usually sold in the Mexican or "ethnic" section of the supermarket), a chopped onion, some minced garlic, some dried oregano, bay leaf some fresh or dried whole mild to medium chilies (California or New Mexican style), ground chili powder or flakes (depending on your hotness preference). You can also get the smoky flavor and the heat by using chipotle peppers (smoked jalopenos) usually sold in a can in "adobo" sauce. If you want, some shredded cabbage as a garnish.

- I usually throw everything, except the hominy, into a big kettle of salted water and cook for a few hours until you have a nice rich smelling broth and the meat is very tender.
- If using a chicken carcass or fresh chicken parts, strain the soup, pull the meat off the bones and return meat to the broth.
- Add the hominy to the broth and meat and finish cooking.
- Adjust salt and pepper.

This soup is "as good as it gets"!

Onion Soup a la Julia

Actually, "it" doesn't get any better than this simple concoction which may be one of the most classic and basic of all soups. The true "peasant's" repast. Yes, as Patrick would say go ahead and use canned broth, if that's all you have. But if you want to taste the real thing make your own broth. I make mine by first of all having homemade beef broth on hand. To do this, ask your friendly neighborhood meat department or butcher for "beef soup bones", or what they have left over from trimming expensive cuts of beef. The more "chi-chi" stores bundles them up in a plastic bag, throw them in the frozen meat case and call them "dog bones". Whatever.

> 🍽 Take them home, put them on a cookie sheet and roast them in the oven. Then take the roasted bones and boil them for hours in plenty of water and trimmings from onions, celery, carrot, garlic (basic "odori"). Strain and freeze if you're not using that same day.

INGREDIENTS: Beef broth, onions, salt, sugar, white wine or dry white vermouth, a baguette, a tasty meltable cheese (such as Gruyere, Swiss, or Emmenthaler), oil, butter, salt, pepper.

- Slice a lot of onions very thin.
- Cook them in a heavy covered pot with a little butter and olive oil over low heat for several minutes until they're nice and soft.
- Take the cover off and sprinkle in a few pinches of salt and sugar, turn up the heat a little and cook for a while, stirring often, until the onions are all a nice deep golden brown.
- Add a little flour and stir continually until well incorporated with the onions, and the flour has browned slightly.
- Pour in the wine and stir up the onions, scraping up whatever has stuck to the bottom of the pot.
- Add the warm broth and simmer for a while until the soup is a slightly thickened mass of melted onions and broth.
- Taste for salt and pepper.
- While soup is simmering, toast some baguette slices, and fit them into the bottom of large bowls in one layer.
- Ladle soup over the "croutons" and sprinkle a handful of grated cheese over.

You can serve like that, while the cheese melts into the hot soup, or stick the bowls into a warm oven for a little while, to let the cheese form a nice covering on top of the soup.

As my brother would say, "soup - it's all in the hand of the cook".

Beans and Bean Soups

John: Note: I used to not care what people said, or what their rationale was, I didn't think you had to soak dried beans overnight. I would sort through them, in their dry state, for pebbles and bad looking beans. And I would rinse them well. But soaking was not necessary, in my opinion. The best rationale I'd seen for pre-soaking was that the swollen bean would tend not to then split during cooking and retain its shape. I used to say, "So what!?". I thought to the contrary, I'd rather have the beans soak up the tasty broth their cooking in, than to soak up a bunch of blah water beforehand.

Patrick: Soaking beans will also shorten the cooking time by semi-tenderizing them and allowing the "blah" absorbed water to heat and cook them quicker, therefore speeding the process.

John: First you must define the word, "blah". I did agree with the concept of soaking as a way to shorten the actual cooking cycle. But for example, if you decided to cook beans for dinner one night, and forgot to start soaking them the day before, don't sweat it. It isn't really necessary, since you can speed up the soaking process by soaking in boiled water, with a lid on the pot, for an hour before using them in a recipe. I actually remember reading something somewhere about this whole soaking issue, now that I recall, that said most beans raised these days are hybrids that don't require soaking. That in days gone by, the beans had a harder skin that required soaking. But before we both beat this particular horse to a complete pulp, let me simply say (and correct myself):

> You **must** pre-soak dried in cold water for at least 12 hours, or boil in water for 5 minutes, and then let soak in the boiled water for another hour. This is especially true of red kidney beans and cannellini (white kidney beans), but is also generally true of black, pinto, fava, navy, and so on.

I discovered this when doing some Internet research on why some people have various digestive reactions to beans. Anyway, beans contain a compound called lectin, which can be toxic if not neutralized by soaking. In some people like me (especially those of European heritage) the toxicity can be potentially more than simply annoying. In almost all people it can at the very least be the root cause of excessive gas or cramps.

A Tuscan Bean Soup

INGREDIENTS: Dried white (soaked and drained) beans, pancetta or salt pork, garlic, olive oil, fresh rosemary, bread, small dried pasta.

- Cook beans in a lot of water, together with a chunk of pancetta and some whole peeled garlic cloves until the beans are tender.
- Drain, saving the liquid, and put through a food mill.
- Put puree back into pot and warm up, adding cooking water until you have nice consistency.
- Warm some olive oil in a frying pan. Toast some bread slices in the oil, and then add some fresh rosemary to the oil and sauté it a few minutes.
- Pour the oil into the soup.
- Add some small dried pasta shells, elbows, or tubetti to the soup and simmer until the pasta is done.
- Put a toasted bread slice in each bowl and ladle over a serving of soup.

If you want to serve this soup cold the next day, cook the toast slices in the soup while the pasta is cooking.

> 🍽 **Tuscan and bean note:** *Tuscans are called the "bean-eaters" because beans are such a staple in their diet. The typical bean is the cannellini, but you'll also see borlotti, ceci, navy, great northern, pinto, and others.*

A Version of Pasta e' Fagioli

INGREDIENTS: Onion, garlic, prosciutto, broth, dried beans, a potato, crushed tomatoes, fresh rosemary, small dried pasta, parmigiano.

- Sauté some chopped onion, garlic, and prosciutto in some olive oil, in a soup pot.
- Add broth, dried cannellini, a diced potato, some canned crushed or diced tomatoes, and some fresh rosemary – cook until beans are almost done.
- Add some small pasta and finish cooking the soup.
- Sprinkle grated parmigiano and fresh salt and pepper on each bowlful.

Farro and Bean Soup

This a Tuscan soup that is as earthy, basic, and satisfying as you can possibly get. You can just picture the early Etruscans slurping this soup, sitting in their abodes on the hill in Fiesole, outside of what is now Florence. Farro is the whole berry of soft spring wheat, sometimes called "spelt". It is not hard to find, especially in stores that offer bulk foods. The accompanying bean is the cannellini.

INGREDIENTS: Cannellini (though I'm now using small white navy beans since I've discovered my mild allergy to kidney beans, of which cannellini are the white version), farro, carrot, onion, celery, garlic, pancetta or prosciutto, chicken broth (or vegetable), salt and pepper, olive oil.

Basic proportions are 1 C farro: 1 C bean: 3 Q(uarts) broth.

- Chop the odori and meat.
- Put the chopped stuff into a soup pot with the soaked/drained beans and broth.
- Cook, covered, until the beans are tender.
- Here you can either puree the beans (traditional) or not.
- Add soaked and rinsed farro and cook until the wheat berries open.

Serve either warm or room temp with a drizzle of olive oil and some pepper.

Black Bean Soup

Alas, a more Mexican or Southwestern concoction, but it fits the classic, peasant, simple mold.

INGREDIENTS: Dried black beans, cumin seed, coriander seed, dried oregano, onion, garlic, jalapeños (or whatever degree of hot you want – you might dry some chipotles in adobo sauce for that smokiness), cilantro, bay, thyme, pepper, tomato puree, salt.

- You can tie all the herbs, spices, and odori up in a cheesecloth bundle if you want – or not (just chop them and add) – and put them in a large stock pot with the soaked and drained beans, plenty of water, and a little tomato puree.
- Simmer for hours until done.

Make as thick (cook down and/or puree some of the cooked soup) or thin (add more liquid) as you like.

Beans in olive oil, salt, pepper, and rosemary

JOHN: Here is one of my favorite summertime dinner recipes. Sometimes just this, a green salad, and some crusty bead will suffice for the whole meal. White wine, or a nice rose' aren't bad either. Ideally, you would use leftover room temp cannellini cooked in a flask. However, this is often a wintertime recipe because the beans cook all day on the stove, creating a lot of heat in the kitchen. So, here's where I'll use canned cannellini (don't let Patrick know I do this).

INGREDIENTS: Canned cannellini, good fruity virgin olive oil, salt, pepper, sprigs or fresh rosemary.

- Rinse and drain the canned beans well in a colander.
- Put in a serving bowl.
- Pour the oil over.
- Sprinkle with salt and pepper.
- Slip in some fresh rosemary leaves.
- Let sit for a while to allow the rosemary flavor to infuse the beans.

Eat at room temperature.

Beans – with sage, garlic, and tomato

INGREDIENTS: Dried beans, garlic, fresh sage, tomato puree, broth.

- Sauté some garlic and fresh sage leaves in some olive oil.
- Add some tomato puree.
- Add some broth and beans.
- Simmer until done.
- Add fresh ground salt and pepper.

These may be cooked down, left "soupy", or baked to eat as a side dish. You can also cook them with a chunk of pancetta, salt pork, or prosciutto for more flavoring.

> I guess the idea is, soup is a mélange of stuff you have, that you like, cooked together to your taste. Soup is the ultimate medium to do what you like and experiment with. Fortunately, or unfortunately, you may never be able to cook the same brew twice.

Baked Beans

Patrick: This is a typical Boston baked bean recipe.

INGREDIENTS: Soaked great northern beans, bacon cut up, chopped onion, chopped garlic, brown sugar, catsup, maple syrup, dark molasses, Worcestershire sauce, salt & pepper.

- Drain and rinse beans and put them in a pot , cover with water and bring to boil.
- Cover and simmer until tender but still firm.
- Drain the water but reserve it for later.
- In a Dutch oven sauté the bacon until crisp and the fat is rendered.
- Add the onion and garlic and cook until tender.
- Add the brown sugar and dissolve.
- Add the catsup, syrup, molasses, Worcester, salt & pepper.
- Bring to a slow boil and then add the drained beans and mix together.
- Add a little of the reserved bean water.
- Cover and put in a low/medium oven.
- Check every now and then. Stir and add more bean water if becoming too thick.

This whole cooking process will take a few hours until the beans are very tender. The end product should be thick when served but not such that it will stick to a spoon when you turn it upside down.

John: You can "live on beans and soup". Take my word for it.

Patrick: So I wonder why John doesn't just eat beans and soup?

John: Well, it's all that soaking business ….

Risotti

John: I guess technically this should be in the pasta chapter, but I'm giving it its own section. It's really more of a one act play, thought the interpretations are infinite.

Patrick: You should know that when making a risotto, that it's not one of those dishes you can walk away from and let simmer. You need to pay close attention to the absorption of the broth which can happen very quickly, adding more as needed. Stirring is very frequent and heat should be no more than medium/low. Although a simple enough dish, you *must* pay attention as it cooks. A final note on this is to learn the basic risotto before moving on with further experimentation. By the way, my wife has become the official risotto cook of the house.

John: You must use a good, imported Italian Arborio rice. It's a fattish, roundish grain.

Patrick: If John was a grain that is what he would be.

John: And of course Pat would be an *Uncle Ben's Converted* (or rather *Per*verted) grain.

The Basic Basic risotto proportions are about 3 cups of broth to a cup of Arborio.

INGREDIENTS: Meat broth, onion, butter, oil, dry white wine, Arborio rice, parmigiano.

- Heat meat broth (chicken, beef, veal) in a saucepan.
- Chop a little onion up very fine.
- Sautee the onion in a little melted butter and some olive oil in another, larger saucepan.
- Pour in a cup of rice, and stir to warm and coat the grains with oil and butter mixture.
- Pour in a little white wine, and let it mostly evaporate away while stirring.
- Add about a half cup of hot broth at a time to the rice, stirring it in until it is absorbed.
- Keep adding half cups of broth, stirring, until the rice is cooked (al dente).
- At this point, it's up to personal taste if the risotto should be a little soupy (but not thin or brothy) or stiffer. But the grains should not be mushy or lose their identity. If anything a little chewy.
- Turn off the heat and swirl in a little more butter and some grated cheese until they're melted and incorporated into the risotto.
- Salt and pepper to taste.

The Milanese Variant

• Add some saffron to the broth.

Patrick: although John does not list this as the "basic" risotto, it is the most common. Saffron should be used sparingly not only because it is expensive but also a little packs a lot of flavor. You can always add more but you can't take out what you've already put in. Also, I like to use a mortar and pestle to grind the strands before adding. By the way, store your saffron in the refrigerator.

The Venetian Variant

• Substitute some chopped parsley, celery, and pancetta for the onion.
• Add some fresh or good frozen green peas with the last half cup of broth.

My Variant

• Use leftover fish soup broth (spicy, tomatoey or otherwise).
• Omit cheese.

You get the point. Play with it. Everything's fair game. Sausages, mushrooms, asparagus, artichokes ……. Kinda like soup. But like with pasta, the rice is the star, so don't kill it.

Braising Meat

John: Whatever the precise culinary definition of "braising" is, doesn't concern me here. For the purpose of this monologue, it's about taking typically less costly cuts of meat and cooking them in a flavorful liquid of some kind, for a long time.

It could be a whole, or pieces of, chicken which may take an hour or less. Or a lamb or beef shank, oxtail, or short ribs which take several hours. Or a piece of tripe (cow's stomach lining) which may take literally all day or all night. There is a definite, sublime pleasure in buying the least expensive meat cuts in a good meat market or meat department of a good grocery store and with very little effort and no gourmet culinary tricks, turn them into one of the most satisfying, impressive, and delicious meals you can ever cook.

Having said that, I usually save braising for cooler weather months because it means having the oven on for several hours, which warms the kitchen considerably, and often entails the use of winter vegetables like carrots, turnips, and potatoes – though not always.

Braising has several steps. Sounds intimidating, but unless you've done it, you don't realize how simple and effortless it is:

- Pre-heat the oven to no more than 300F.
- Dry the meat well, so it will brown properly, and cut if you desire into whatever serving sizes you wish, though it's not absolutely necessary since you can do this after it's cooked.
- Brown the meat well in hot fat in a heavy pot, preferably a cast iron Dutch oven with a close fitting heavy lid. Use your favorite fat, or one that works best with the dish you have in mind.
- Remove the browned meat and pouring out most of the excess fat.
- Brown odori, if you wish to use them.
- Return meat to pot and add wine, which is then boiled off by about half.
- Add whatever other ingredients you wish to eat, or to simply flavor the broth and meat.
- Add more cooking liquid, such as broth, water, mushroom liquor, etc. to almost cover the meat.
- Bring the pot to a simmer on the stove top.
- Cover the pot tightly with the lid.
- Stick the pot in the oven for as long as it takes to cook the meat sufficiently.
- Do something else while the meat cooks.
- Check once in a while to make sure the liquid is only barely simmering, but not boiling, and adding more boiling liquid if necessary to keep the original level up. You may also want to add vegetables, that you want to be flavored with the liquid, later, after the meat has cooked a while.
- Remove pot from oven and remove the meat and vegetables.
- Skim off almost all the fat that's floating on the surface of the liquid.
- Boil the remaining liquid down to a condensed, thicker version of itself, or whisk in a thickener like a flour or cornstarch paste.
- Return meat and vegetables to pot to re-heat.

| If you want to eat this time-consuming dish during the middle of the week, when you don't have the time, then make it over the weekend and put it in the fridge with the fat still floating on the surface. Then when you're ready to re-heat, just lift the hardened excess fat from the surface and throw away. Saves time skimming when the dish is hot.

Here are a couple of recipe ideas to get you started. Then when you've got the hang of it, experiment to perfect your masterpiece which will impress everyone, every time.

Veal (or beef or lamb) shanks (or oxtails or short ribs) braised in red wine, tomato, broth, and odori. (This is more typical of an Italian type "Osso Buco" in flavorings)

INGREDIENTS: Odori vegetables, meat shanks (or short ribs, oxtails, pot roast, etc.), red wine, beef broth, dried porcini, crushed tomatoes (or chopped fresh or tomato puree), your secret flavorings.

- Brown the meat and remove.
- Add finely shopped carrot, parsley, celery, garlic, and onion to the pot, and brown them lightly.
- Return meat to pot and add red wine. Boil it down about half, to remove alcohol and leave the wine's essence.
- Add beef broth and liquor from soaking dried porcini mushrooms.
- Chop the mushrooms and add.
- Add some crushed tomatoes or tomato paste. Not too much if you don't want the broth too tomatoey, which you don't.
- Add some salt.
- (You might be tempted to add some secret ingredient like a star anise, or some vin santo, or an anchovy, or some bay, or whatever at this point. "Who's to know?").
- Bring to simmer, cover, put in oven, etc.
- Salt and pepper to your taste before you serve. Maybe a little grated orange zest. You're the cook!
- Put a shank on each plate and ladle some of the thickened, unstrained sauce over it.

Bread is good to sop up the broth. You may want to serve this with some creamy polenta also.

Lamb shanks (or chunks of boned lamb shoulder) braised in white wine, beans, and olives. (This is flavored like a Provençal style stew)

Again, I take my cue from Erick for these flavorings, by I completely absolve him from my bastardizing of his recipes.

INGREDIENTS: Boned lamb shoulder, tomato paste or crushed tomatoes, carrot, turnip, dried white beans, celery, un-pitted olives, bay leaf, garlic, nutmeg, other secret herbs of your choice, white wine, broth.

- After browning the lamb, add a tad of tomato paste or a small amount of crushed tomatoes, some carrots and turnips cut in chunks, some dried white beans, some chopped celery, some black or green (or both) unpitted olives, some bay leaves, some chopped garlic, and grate in a little bit of a whole nutmeg.
- Here's your chance to sneak in a secret ingredient or two – maybe some thyme branches tied in a bundle with some string.
- Pour in white wine to almost cover and boil it down some to remove some alcohol.
- Add some water or vegetable broth to re-fill the liquid level.
- Add some salt.
- Simmer, cover, stick in the oven, etc.
- Reduce the liquid, if you wish or if necessary, when the meat is done.
- Season to your taste with salt and pepper.
- Serve from the pot onto plates or into large bowls, depending on the thickness of the liquid.

Bread of course to sop up liquid.

Remind your guests that the olives still have the pits in them. Whoever gets the bag of herbs is the winner. Just kidding. Take it out before serving.

Chicken braised in red wine and herbs with pancetta (This is basically the classic Coq au Vin of French repute)

INGREDIENTS: Cut-up chicken parts, butter, pancetta, cognac, red wine, stock, garlic, thyme, bay leaf, tomato paste, butter, flour.

- Brown the very dry chicken pieces in butter, in which some chopped pancetta has been previously browned. I recommend using the more flavorful dark meat like legs and thighs, and not using the insipid white meat breasts.
- Add some cognac, if you wish, to the pot and carefully ignite it to burn away the alcohol.
- Pour in red wine to cover chicken and boil away the alcohol.
- Pour in chicken or beef stock to bring liquid level back up.
- Add some garlic, thyme, bay leaves, and tomato paste.
- Bring to simmer, cover, stick in oven until the chicken is cooked to your satisfaction.
- Remove from oven, skim fat, discard bay, remove chicken from pot and whip in a butter/flour paste to thicken the liquid.
- Return chicken to pot, to blend with the sauce, and re-heat.
- Salt and pepper to your taste before serving.

Typically this may be served with sautéed mushroom, and whole small onions browned in butter and braised in a covered skillet on top of the stove with some beef stock and herbs.

Braciole (brah-cho-lay)

Braciole means thin slices of meat. The recipes made from braciole are also called braciole.

> 🍽 *A braciola recipe is just a thin slice of meat (e.g. a butterflied beef sirloin, or a boneless and skinless chicken breast, etc. pounded thinner between waxed paper) stuffed with a filling of chopped and usually sauteed vegetables, cheese, etc., rolled up and tied with twine, browned in a heavy pan. Liquid is added, and braised, covered, until tender. Thin fish fillets can also be used, but without the pounding process. Unless you're using one hell of a tough fish.*

This is a whole genre that you can experiment with, and possibly make one of your own signature dishes.

Patrick: Essentially, if you have a less than a desirable piece of meat there is always something to do with it and the braising or long simmering as Johnny notes is pretty much the way to go. Whether you end up eating that piece of meat as a large whole or in pieces or even the broth created from it, you will sure to have a positive result. So remember, don't necessarily bypass those cheap cuts in the butcher shop because the creative mind can always turn a sow's ear into a silk purse.

John: Hmmmm ..... braised sows' ears.

Roasting, Barbecuing, and Grilling

John: Basically the rule that governs the central theme of this book, which is "keep it simple and clean" (i.e. by "clean" I mean doing as little as possible to your main ingredient by way of saucing, marinating, etc.), applies especially to roasting, barbecuing, and grilling. Once again I emphasize buying high-quality, un-drugged, grass-fed, free-range beasts – especially if you're not going to over-douse it with stuff. Remember that before the time of refrigeration, meats that were grilled or roasted often were not at the peak of their freshness, causing sea-going nations to seek routes to the Indies for the spices necessary to cover up the foul taste of spoiling meat. So too in this age, it's necessary to cover up the taste of meats that are essentially "manufactured" in factory-like settings and sold in huge national grocery store chains and in cheap "steak and brew" restaurant chains.

🍽 *A note here about my bias toward organic, grass-fed, etc. meat – I am not a true organic freak by nature, nor am I (obviously) a vegan or vegetarian. People have their own reasons for not eating meat, or avoiding dairy or wheat, or whatever. And that's their business, especially if there are strongly held moral, religious, cultural, or health reasons involved. I espouse the "whole foods" theory of meat and vegetables because they simply taste better, are often free of chemical coatings (which can't taste good or be good for you), and generally don't carry e-coli bacterium (and others) on their bodies or in their guts. And buying locally, in general is not so much about sustaining local farmers, as it is about buying fresh and knowing where your food comes from. In other words, I'm practical about what I put into my mouth, chew, and swallow.*

OK. So you've got your good quality leg of lamb, pork loin, rib-eye steak, roaster chicken, baby back ribs, rabbit, goose, or duck at home. Now what? When time allows, I'll generally dry it with paper towels, douse it with some kosher salt, lay it on a rack, uncovered, lay the rack on a cookie sheet, and place the whole thing in the refrigerator for a day or two. Somehow this tenderizes the meat and keeps it juicier during cooking. Really! No kidding? Doesn't make intuitive sense, but somehow it changes the chemistry of the meat. If time doesn't allow, I of course skip this process and go straight to the flame, though even some time using this dry brining works better than none at all. Here are some recipe ideas for different kinds of meats for roasting, grilling, or barbecuing.

Bistecca alla Fiorentina –
the signature dish of Tuscany

INGREDIENTS: Porterhouse or t-bone a good 2 inches thick, salt, pepper.

- Build a hot hardwood charcoal fire (preferably), but a gas grill that gets very hot will do, if that's all you can muster, (or grill under a very hot broiler in your oven as a last resort).
- When the coals are all fiery red (no black un-burned charcoal to be seen) and starting to get ashen, put the steak on with tongs or a spatula (not a fork which will puncture the meat) and grill the first side until it's just barely charred.
- Flip over with the tongs or spatula and do the other side.
- The steak must be exceedingly rare!
- Take the steak off and salt it with plenty of fresh ground salt.
- Knock the excess salt off, and grind some pepper on the steak.
- Put it on a plate and eat it.

This also works especially well with very thick veal chops, if you can find a non-politically correct butcher.

Once I heard, or read, a variation on this, which was to pour some hot olive oil, in which some fresh rosemary had been steeped, over the finished steak. It's not the purist's recipe, but it's also a "clean" option.

Barbecued Baby Back Ribs

INGREDIENTS: Marinade makings (see below), baby back ribs (or any kind of ribs, brisket, etc.)

- Make some type of steaming liquid which serves your own tastebuds well. (I use a little high-sodium soy, maybe a little brown sugar, some salt and pepper, maybe a little balsamic vinegar, and some olive oil.) Whatever you concoct, it should be liquidy, not thick.
- Line a cookie sheet, that has raised edges, with foil.
- Place the uncooked ribs on the foil and pour the cooking liquid over.
- Cover the sheet with more foil and seal the top foil to the bottom by crimping the edges together.
- Put into a slow oven for a few hours.
- Build a hardwood charcoal fire, or turn on only one side of your gas grill. (or, alas, turn on your oven to high.)
- Push the coals to one the sides of the barbecue. I, by the way, use a Weber kettle drum shaped barbecue with bottom and top vents.
- Put the ribs on the grill, but not directly over the coals.
- Brush them with some of the cooking liquid.
- Put the top securely on the barbecue, and open both the bottom and tops vents.
- Cook until the ribs are well glazed and smoked, but not dried out or charred.

This method ensures moist, sticky, fall-off-the-bone tender ribs. Experiment with cooking liquids, but try to keep them clean and simple. Herbs work well – sage maybe. Maybe some sweet vermouth. Whatever makes it uniquely "you".

Chicken Feast – it's too simple to say I invented it, but I think I did

INGREDIENTS: A whole roasting chicken, salt.

- Rinse and dry the whole chicken.
- If time allows, this is an especially good recipe for salting and curing the chicken for a day or two, as I described above.
- Brush off (don't rinse) the excess salt before roasting.
- Build the charcoal fire, as in the rib recipe above, and push the coals to the side (or use a hot-ish oven).
- If you want you can lightly rub the chicken with a little oil or butter, but not a lot. I usually just add some fresh ground sea salt.
- Place the chicken on the grill, but not directly over the coals.
- Pit the grill's lid on, with top and bottom vents open.
- If the grill stays hot, go do something else for an hour.
- Come back and take the chicken off the grill, put it on a platter, and serve it.

Sometimes I like to serve the chicken with a little Dijon mustard as a condiment. Or I may serve as a condiment a little Major Grey's sweet mango chutney. In any case, save and freeze the carcass, And one day when you have time, boil it in lots of water with some frozen onion, carrot, and celery trimmings that you've saved from other recipes, for several hours. Strain the broth and freeze in yogurt containers. This makes a great smoky base for soups later on.

Some other chicken variations I like (though to tell the truth I'm not a huge chicken fan, and prefer a roast duck)

- Stick some fresh herbs inside the chicken before roasting. Tarragon? Sage? Rosemary?
- Sprinkle some mesquite, or applewood, or oak, or olive wood chips soaked in water for a few minutes over the coals before putting the top on the barbecue. This adds flavor and gives the skin a mahogany color.
- Stuff some course Italian semi-stale bread chunks, which have been soaked in some oil, vinegar, and herbs, under the chicken's skin before roasting.

Arista – pork roast flavored with garlic and rosemary (a Tuscan classic, also)

INGREDIENTS: A boneless pork roast (butterflied), garlic, rosemary, olive oil, salt, and pepper. Kitchen string.

- Make a mixture or chopped coarsely chopped garlic, fresh rosemary, fresh ground salt, and pepper.
- Open up the roast and spread the mixture around inside.
- Close up the roast and truss it up well with kitchen string.
- Make some small slits with the tip of a sharp knife on the outside of the trussed roast and stuff some garlic slivers into the slits.
- Rub the roast with olive oil.
- As with the chicken and ribs above barbecue (not directly over the coals) roast the pork with lid on, or in a medium/hot oven until it's just past the pink stage inside (use a meat thermometer) so that it doesn't dry out and lose its juicy flavor.
- Un-truss and slice into pieces crosswise. If you roasted in the oven on a rack in a roasting pan (or if you trapped the drippings by placing a pan in your barbecue under the meat), deglaze the drippings with some sweet vermouth and use it as a sauce.

Sausages

Buy fresh, not smoked or pre-cooked, house-made sausages from the good butcher or meat department of a good market. Although many would argue that chicken or turkey sausages are "better for you", pork sausages are far better tasting, and certainly more traditional. Still, I've tasted a lot of variations on fowl-based sausage and many of them are quite good. Either way, good sausage is made with 2 parts meat to 1 part fat, and I don't think that chicken fat is "healthier" for you than pork fat. Suit yourself.

- Put the sausages in a skillet and add a little water to about a third of the way up the sausages.
- Cook the sausages, turning a few times, until they're essentially steamed done throughout, the water has simmered away, and some fat has rendered out of the sausages.
- Turn up the heat a little and lightly brown the sausages in their own rendered fat.
- Leave the heat on, and put the sausages on a serving platter.
- Pour some sweet vermouth into the hot pan and deglaze the drippings, scraping up any burned on particles of meat or fat.
- Reduce the sauce to a medium thick "syrup", and pout it over the sausage.
- Serve with Dijon mustard, or just the de-glazed reduction, or whatever you like.

I like to soak up the sauce with French or Italian bread.

Grilled Sausages

Patrick: These are pork based sausages I am referring to. I am not concerned with all the other nonsense out there. Ideally, your sausages should come as coiled rope style. Also, I find the best are stuffed in sheep casing which are much narrower than beef casing which you normally see at a market. Sausage stuffed in sheep casing are about the diameter of your thumb, roughly. If they are not skewered for you then do it yourself as it makes turning the whole rope at one time much easier.

- Take your sausage rope and place on you top rack over direct heat.
- Your first 2-3 flips of the rope should be within a few minutes of each other.
- After that watch for grease to form in the crevices in the ring.
- When it does, flip and watch for the grease again.
- When there is just a little grease left rising then the sausage is done.

Nice served with fresh squeezed lemon.

Roast Christmas Goose

I've gotten into the habit of doing a roast goose for Christmas instead of turkey – because it tastes better, it's more traditional, it doesn't leave you with mountains of leftover meat, it's a change of pace from the Thanksgiving turkey, and you can use the rendered goose fat (liters of it!) to deep fry potatoes (if you *must* deep fry something).

INGREDIENTS: A whole goose (they normally come frozen and often you have to pre-order them), stuffing (rice, apples, prunes, figs, herbs, etc.).

- Stuff the goose loosely with some apples, prunes, figs, herbs, cooked wild rice – whatever.
- Roast it. Some folks will boil the goose somewhat before roasting, I guess to render some of the huge quantities of fat.
- Make gravy by first removing most of the copious amount of rendered fat, browning some flour in the remaining fat, and stirring in boiling water, a little a time, until the gravy meets your desired consistency.
- Salt and pepper the gravy until your heart's content.

Patrick: Yes, folks, this needs to be here, as great burgers are not just something as benign as a hot dog.

Hamburgers

INGREDIENTS: Ground chuck, salt & pepper.

The chuck has a higher fat content (20%) and this where the flavor comes from.

- Loosely form hamburger patties and I mean loosely. Do not pack them! Form them gently just they stay together and form a patty.
- To grill, place on a hot fire. Do not press them down with a spatula or similar or you will release the juices and the burger will dry out.
- Typically, you only need to flip them once.
- A simple press with your finger will tell you their doneness; soft: rare, soft/firm: medium, firm: well done.

What you do with them after they come off the grill is your decision.

Summary

As you can see, the meats in these recipes are the stars, and their preparations are simple, consistent, and honest. Furthermore, the recipes are easy to throw together quickly, and they require very little attention during cooking. This is every day cooking that you can do any day of the week. You could for instance, oven-steam the ribs on Sunday while you're reading the *Sunday New York Times Magazine,* and barbecue them later in the week. Most of these meats can be roasted in the oven in an hour or less, while you're having a Cosmo or a glass of wine, or blanching and sautéing some kale, broccolirab, or chard. Just replace some of your post work day time that you'd normally spend watching canned news on "Fox", with some quality cooking time. It might also be a good time for you to connect with your partner, as long as he cooks his own recipe, or otherwise stays out of your way. And the kids can help, or they can just shut up and go do their homework. And remember, if they don't like what you cook, then they should sit at the table anyway and just go hungry. And you'll pledge to yourself that in your next life you'll bring up your kids from scratch with a trained palate instead of a mac n' cheese and hot dog obsession.

Seafood

John: In my experience, fish can be simple or impossible. It takes a real specialist to get fish right, consistently. That's why restaurants who do fish very, very well are usually places that more or less specialize in seafood. I am always searching for the basic fish preparation that satisfies my culinary standards, but there are certain criteria for buying and cooking fish that should never be fiddled with:

• You must buy the very freshest fish from a place that has a good reputation for seafood, and that sells a lot of it (there's that "quick turn" criterion again). However, in some cases you may see a sign on a piece of fish that it has been "previously frozen at sea", or in fact the fish may be frozen at the time you buy it. I've never totally satisfied myself as to whether freezing fish is bad, in general. Though in some cases I can see that it may be good. I would think that freezing any kind of delicate fish, say like sole, may destroy the tender flesh, and in fact I never see this type of fish frozen, at least in good markets. For fish that must be eaten as soon as possible after it leaves the sea, such as mackerel (because it's oily and can spoil very quickly) I often see them frozen whole or in fillets. Though freezing may in fact do some damage to the structure of the flesh, the upside is that it preserves the oily integrity of the fish, otherwise we would rarely eat an oily fish since it's very hard to get from sea to table as quickly as it requires. The other rule-breaker for the fresh factor is of course baccala, or salt cod, which is a food in its own separate right. I recommend strongly looking for fresh fish in Asian markets that handle a lot of fish , especially Japanese fish markets. Often, Asian markets actually have the live fish swimming in big tanks. They'll kill and clean it while you wait. And if you cook it that same night, it can't get any fresher.

• Price does not always directly correlate with quality. Price has more to do with the supply of a given seafood, and the cost of harvesting and distributing it. It also has to do with the "sexiness" of a type of fish and how attractive it presents itself in the case. A "mahi-mahi" steak looks and sounds a lot more exotic than a whole grotesque rockfish or a dark, bloody-looking albacore tuna loin. Freshness and quality have more to do with what's in season, close to you.

• Don't buy farmed seafood, in general, especially fish or shrimp. It doesn't taste as good. It is fed artificial stuff, is laden with antibiotics to retard the spread of fishy diseases in the densely packed "fish corrals", and is even injected with dyes as in the case of farm-raised salmon. Also, farming fish raises serious pollution issues in the areas they're farmed, such as lagoons, marshes, and estuaries. The major exception to the farming factor is, in my mind, oysters. Oysters can carry harmful parasites and other bad toxins, especially if they're "wild". Farming them to a very large degree can greatly control disease and other bad things that can transmit be transmitted to humans.

• Unless you're very confident of the seafood's origins and its handling, don't eat it raw. I do eat sushi, but only at places that have a good, and spotless, reputation. If I make sushi at home, I buy the fresh fish from a fish market that offers the quality and expertise that can help ensure its safety. Raw oysters are always a potential risk, but once again, knowing and trusting their source can alleviate some of the risk.

• I don't know of any seafood that should be cooked very long, with the exception of a whole, large octopus. Fish is delicate, subtle, and when fresh it is divine. Therefore it should never be overcooked, over-sauced, or over-handled.

• Eat fish as often as you can, within the constraints of your budget, the variety's tendency to harbor toxicity, and your ability to get the freshest possible. It's good for you, cooks in no time, and has very little waste.

Here some recipe examples, using different types of fish and cooking methods. These will give you a varied repertoire that you can personalize and expand from.

Grilled Norwegian Mackerel Fillets

I see them often pre-filleted, and frozen in the good Asian markets I shop at. Keep them frozen until the day you plan to eat them. As with any frozen fish, don't keep it frozen long. It will quite quickly become unusable left frozen too long.

INGREDIENTS: Fresh or frozen mackerel fillets or whole cleaned mackerel, Dijon mustard, lemon.

- Take the fillets (if frozen), usually vacuum sealed, out of the freezer, keep them in their store packaging, place the package in another tightly sealed plastic bag, and put the bag into the refrigerator. In the evening, un-package them and dry them out well on paper towels. Cook all fresh fish, especially oily fish, the day you buy it.
- Over hot hardwood charcoal coals, or under a hot broiler, grill them quickly, to the degree of doneness you prefer, but don't overdo it. Seafood's flavor and texture is quickly ruined once it's overdone.
- Serve with a light brushing of Dijon mustard, and/or some lemon juice, or maybe a little brushing of a lemon, garlic puree, and salt vinaigrette.

Of course this method works well with whole, cleaned, sardines, if you can find them. Or with Eastern bluefish, or any other similar fish

> 🍽 *I have also seen ideas for oily fish where they are simmered, or poached, in liquids, such as a mixture of soy, sherry, ginger, garlic, and rice vinegar.*

Seared Salmon, Tuna, Halibut Fillets or Steaks

INGREDIENTS: Fish steaks or fillets, olive oil, salt, sugar, dry hot Oriental mustard.

- Pre-heat your oven to very hot.
- Dry the fish well and brush on a little bit of olive oil, on the flesh side only if it's a fillet.
- Heat up a very heavy cast iron skillet over a high flame. It's best to turn on your exhaust fan if you have one.
- Prepare a little paste with some water, salt, dry Oriental (hot) mustard, and some sugar.
- Sear both sides of a steak, or just the flesh side of a fillet, very briefly.
- Flip the fillet onto its skin side and brush the top lightly with the paste.
- Pop the grill into the hot oven and finish cooking until it's done to your liking.
- Please don't overcook it. The flesh should say moist inside. Salmon should even *look* a little rare inside, as the outside tends to lighten in color as it cooks. Trial and error will perfect your timing, to suit your personal preference.

> **|◎| Note:** *Alternatively (to the mustard, sugar, water glaze) I've been using a pureed garlic, lemon juice, Dijon, salt, pepper, and olive oil mixture (whisked into a state of semi-thickness) as a topping for the grilled or seared fish. You could go ahead and also make the aioli with some egg yolk, a la Erick.*

Often times, when you serve a fillet this way, the flesh will pull away from the skin very easily when you eat or serve it. With salmon fillets usually I pull out any little bones with needle nose pliers before I cook them. It makes for a more pleasant dining experience, especially for kids. For tuna, when it's in season, I go for the whole albacore tuna loin. I slice it into very thick (1.5 inches) slabs across the grain of the loin before I cook them. I usually have to tie a piece of kitchen string around the middle of each piece to keep it from "un-layering" itself. As far as saucing fish cooked simply like this, especially if it's a little more oily or flavorful, like tuna or salmon, I still try to keep it light and enhance the fish's flavor rather than covering it up. My daughter has invented a light "relish" of fresh diced mango, with a little lime, and cilantro, and a little hint of a fresh chili chopped in. I typically brush a little Dijon on, or maybe dab each forkful into a sweetish Indian chutney like a Major Grey.

Cacciucco (fish soup)

There are as many recipes for fish soup as there are little fishing villages on any coast, anywhere in the world. Cacciucco is a Tuscan seacoast version from Livorno. I'll discuss some variations after this recipe, from other Mediterranean locales. The commonality to probably all the variants around the world is that a stock is prepared of fish trimmings and "ugly" fish, flavored with the local herbs and spices, strained, and fresh seafood added to the resultant broth. Cheese is never, ever used to garnish fish or a seafood soup.

INGREDIENTS: Olive oil, onion, fish trimmings (e.g. heads, skeletons, shrimp shells, cheap "ugly" whole fish like monkfish, small non-oily whole fish, etc.), tomatoes, parsley, hot chilies or hot pepper flakes, red wine vinegar, a combination of fresh seafood to your liking (ocean scallops, halibut, cod, shrimp, cleaned and soaked mussels and clams, etc. but not oily fish).

- Put some olive oil in the bottom of a large stock pot.
- Add some cut up onion and a lot of fish parts (heads, back bones, tails, whole small cleaned fish). Avoid heavier and oily fish. Use cheap rockfish, or whatever other trimmings your fish guy will save for you. Sauté this mixture a little.
- All some chopped tomatoes, some parsley, some chili pepper flakes, and a little red wine vinegar. Cook a little.
- Add water, possibly a little white wine, a tad of vinegar, and some stock. Don't get it heavy tasting.
- Cook until the fish has all fallen apart.
- Put the whole mess through a sieve or food mill in batches.
- Re-heat the resultant rich, spicy, tomatoey, deep-tasting stock.
- Salt and pepper to taste.
- When the stock is up to a simmer, add whatever seafood you want. If shellfish are part of your mix, add them first to give them time to open before you add other fishes. Add for example chunks of halibut or cod, shrimp, sea scallops, etc.
- Cook very briefly just until the seafood turns barely opaque, and the shellfish are opened.
- Ladle broth and an assortment of seafood into each person's bowl.
- Often time this type of soup is ladled over a piece of bread, or garlic-rubbed toast which is put in the bottom of each bowl.

If there is any broth left over, or any seafood morsels or particles, save it for making a seafood risotto, later in the week, or freeze it for the same purpose.

Bouillabaisse - style (fish soup from Marseille)

INGREDIENTS: Fish stock as above, tomato, Pernod (or similar "pastis"), thyme, cayenne, garlic, saffron, potato, fresh seafood as above.

- Add some Pernod, some thyme, a little cayenne, some garlic, some saffron to the fish parts when making the stock. Strain.
- Reheat the stock with some cut up potatoes and cook.
- Add seafood and cook briefly.

In this recipe small whole fish are also added to the strained stock, and they are thus served whole. The serving difference is that the seafood and potatoes are removed from the broth and placed on a large platter. Each dinner eats the broth in his own bowl, maybe with a little rouille, again over a garlic rubbed crouton. The fish is eaten separately from the broth.

Another Provençal "Bouillabaisse" Variant

Flavor the broth with onion, garlic, tomato, saffron, thyme, and star anise, and lots of fish parts and small whole fish. Cook slowly for a long time, and put through a food mill. The result is a slightly thick consistency because of the ground up fish flesh. It has a light reddish yellow color from the saffron and the small amount of chopped tomato used.
Ladle the re-heated broth over croutons that have a dollop of fresh made rouille (see pages 65-66) on them. No fresh seafood is added to the finished broth in this recipe. Only the thickish pureed fish broth is served with the rouille and the crouton.

Salt Cod Dip (Brandade)

This is a Provençal recipe also. I like the Provençal style because it is clearly a relative to that of much of Italian cuisine, that is simple, honest, unadorned, and clean. French cooking in general can be very complex, in its combination of flavors and textures, and in its techniques. but not in one of its basic premises is the abundant use of cream and butter. Mai oui! Of course it tastes good! Yes, I do love French classical cooking, but I'll talk more about that later. But for now, back to the "Brandade du Morue." Salt cod is, as I've said above, a food in its own right. Armies traveled on it, civilizations lived on it, and international trade was in part based on it. There are so many recipes, most of which originate in centuries past. Even as early as my own youth, salt cod was still cheap and abundant in stores, especially where fresh seafood wasn't available. It seems that the more typical recipes are some version of a stew, with potatoes and/or tomatoes, or some combination of cod and potatoes in the form of fried balls or patties. So to avoid all that I've chosen an atypical dish to high-light the virtues of baccala.

> 🍽 Salt cod fillets typically come boneless and skinless, and packed in cute little wooden boxes or left whole and unwrapped and sold bulk in old-fashioned Italian delis. In every case they are very well salted and therefore dry and desiccated and must be well rinsed and re-hydrated. You do that by soaking in ample cold water, changed frequently over 24 hours or so. The resultant cod fillets never actually revert totally to the texture and taste of the fresh cod it came from.

INGREDIENTS: Soaked baccala , garlic, salt, lemon juice, ricotta cheese.

- Trim of any skin, thin dry pieces, or anything that looks a little "iffy".
- Poach in plenty of cold water, until just cooked though and tender, then strained and cooled.
- Grate a garlic clove, using a fork as I've described, into a saucer of salt and lemon juice.
- Flake the cooled cod with your fingers into a bowl, and then mash with a fork.
- Mash and stir into the flaked cod some ricotta, the garlic, and some olive oil until you have a nice spreadable "dip".
- Salt to taste.
- Serve on slices of baguette.

Or you can of course mix it with some mashed potatoes, put it in a baking dish, grate some Gruyere on it and bake it. I prefer just the dip thing myself. Even little kids like it. My granddaughter calls it hummus and licks it off her slice of bread, preserving the bread and re-loading the brandade.

Venetian Fried and Marinated Fish

This may be one of the most satisfying fish recipes you can make. It's unique, delicious, simple, and just about everyone likes it. I think Patrick even made it once, and liked it, even though he's not a fish fanatic.

INGREDIENTS: Some sort of firm white skinless and boneless fish (cod, flounder, sole, etc. are all good), eggs, milk, garlic, onion, olive oil pepper, bay leaf, white wine vinegar, pepper, parsley, raisins, pine nuts, bread crumbs (I like to use the unseasoned "panko" style for just about anything I cook that needs to be breaded and fried), canola or corn oil, unsalted butter.

- Cut the fish into fairly uniform serving pieces.
- Marinate them in a mixture of beaten egg, milk, and salt for a little while.
- Cut an onion into thin rings and soak in cold water for a few minutes, then drain.
- "Sweat" (i.e. cook until translucent) the onions in some oil and butter.
- Add salt and pepper, bay leaves, and some vinegar to the onions and sauté.
- Add water to the onions and cook, adding more water as necessary, until you have a nice sauce (i.e. the onions become homogenous and "melt").
- Chop parsley and garlic together.
- Soak raisins.
- Heat vegetable oil and a little butter in a heavy skillet.
- Dip each piece of fish into the crumbs and coat both sides.
- Fry the fish pieces quickly until lightly golden and slightly crispy and lay in a serving dish.
- Pour the onion sauce all over.
- Sprinkle on the garlic, parsley, pine nuts which you may lightly toast in a skillet if you like, drained raisins.
- Cover the dish closely with foil and let marinate and rest for an hour.

Serve without re-heating.

A Provençal Version of Fried Salt Cod

Usually a Christmas Eve dish, traditionally. From Erick's kitchen.

INGREDIENTS: Well-soaked salt cod, olive oil, onion, flour tomatoes, red wine, wine vinegar, garlic, capers, dry-cured black olives, green olives, bay.

- Cut the fish into small serving sized pieces, dip in flour and/or cornstarch, and fry in oil.
- Make a sauce by sautéing chopped onion, garlic, and tomatoes in olive oil.
- Add red wine, a touch of red wine vinegar, capers, bay, and olives.
- Simmer until thickened.
- Pour over fried fish.

Shellfish

Oysters: Are typically eaten raw. I prefer no adornment other then their own salty liquor. Sometimes I like a small dribble of lemon juice. Avoid anything else at all costs. The taste and texture of the critter is what you're after. Some people chew, some don't. It's up to you. Oysters have many different flavor nuances depending on their kind and place of cultivation. They can be briny (Atlantic oysters are saltier than Pacific, because the Atlantic is a saltier ocean), sweet, tasting of seaweed, smoky, tangy, tart, and so on. There's nothing else to say, except sometimes you can roast the larger ones in their shells over coals and eat them cooked. That's OK, too.

Clams and mussels: I put them in fish soups, or as an ingredient in some pasta sauces. But my favorite way to eat these type of shellfish is:

- Soak them in abundant cold water (sea water if you can get some clean sea water) for several hours until they're purged themselves of their last meals and any sand and grit.
- Store them in your refrigerator after you buy them, in a bowl of water or in the plastic bag you brought them home in, but don't seal the bag or you'll suffocate them.
- Drain and rinse them. Trim the beards off mussels.
- Put them in a large shallow pot, which has a lid.
- Add some white wine, some garlic, some oil, or butter, some herbs.
- Put a lid on.
- Steam until they open up. If the shellfish are open before you cook them, or closed after they're cooked, throw them out.
- Eat. Soak up the liquid with bread.

The best way to enjoy this type of recipe is to stand around the pot while it's still on the stove, with your guests or family, and eat communally.

Patrick: I have nothing to add here about fish, since I hate seafood, mostly.

John: Honesty is always the best policy.

Vegetables

John: In fact, my wife and I were "fish-eating vegetarians" for a few years, so vegetables have always been important to our home-grown cuisine. My son, Jeremy, has been a vegetarian, though not vegan for as long as I can remember. He believes that eating meat is a waste of resources, in that the food it takes to raise an animal for slaughter could feed many people. Actually, it's best that I let him explain it here:

Jeremy: Since the turn of my teens at least, I have been deeply concerned about the human toll on the natural environment and the sustainability of our life on earth. For a while, I was an environmental activist and evangelist. With political burnout and a maturing sense of personal responsibility, though, minimizing my own ecological footprint became more important to me than changing public policy or anyone else's mind.

Of course, there are profound reasons for a lifestyle change, and there are proximate causes. At sixteen, my best friend and partner in rabble-rousing Aron had forsworn red meat, for reasons I've now forgotten. (Not least to irritate his mother, I'm sure-- she took his decision very personally for some reason and I recall one absurd argument over whether the veal she'd made for dinner one night was "red" or "white" meat). As in most things, I followed Aron's lead. In the summer I turned seventeen, I spent a few weeks volunteering for the U.S. Forest Service on the Olympic Pensinsula in Washington, where I shared a barracks with a gorgeous hippie chick, a vegan college student who was taking a census of Spotted Owls to prevent their mating grounds being logged. Trying to impress her, I called myself a vegetarian, then admitted that I still ate chicken and fish and... The look of pity she (she who would not taste honey, for it exploits bees) gave me makes me cringe to this day. That was sixteen years ago, and I haven't eaten meat since.

But from catalysts, back to my reasons. I became, and remain, a vegetarian because this diet uses far less natural resources and causes far less pollution than meat-eating. This is because the agricultural-industrial "inputs" that produce the food that I consume directly are a tiny fraction of those needed to produce the equivalent food-value of beef, chicken, pork, catfish or whatever. To grow enough plant-food for one person takes a certain amount of land, water, fertilizer, fuel, and often chemical pesticides and herbicides, plus a share in the vast processing and distribution infrastructure. To "grow" one person's worth of meat takes these resources dozens or hundreds of times over as animals are fed plant-food over a lifetime. You could think of it as nutritional efficiency. It's a short hop from here to just about every environmental issue-- battles over distribution and wise use of land and water resources, pollution from agri-industrial chemicals and waste products (think of those giant pigshit lagoons), global warming from use of fossil fuels, and the sustainability of growing human populations and fragile natural ecosystems. I'm sure there are great statistics to back me up, but frankly I haven't thought about them in years.

(Wild-caught seafood doesn't involve quite the same "efficiency" equation, but large-scale fishing almost always involves massive habitat and population degradation.)

I don't believe it is morally wrong to kill animals for food. To me, eating meat is like driving a Hummer. It's not evil on the scale of rape and murder, but it's frivolous and antisocial. Even that's not a good example, because I'd pick a fight with a Hummer-driver, but I happily share a dinner table and a bed with a carnivore. I do sympathize with people who are vegetarian for other reasons, whether they're animal-rights principles or doctor's orders, but my motivation is just to use and consume less conspicuously. It gives me some peace of mind in this screwed-up world to think that I did a lot less damage than the typical person, that in some convoluted way I made it possible for more people to live longer and better lives. Over the years, though, meat-eating started to seem weird and icky. I may not be a moral absolutist, but an unexpected fishy morsel in my kimchi or bacon in my pea soup makes me gag.

I'm no ascetic; I love to cook and I love to eat. As a 21st-century American I probably have more variety in my diet than 99 percent of the people who have ever lived. I know that by the same eco-logic I should be vegan, but I chose to draw the line at a place where I could balance virtue with convenience and gustatory pleasure. I also have no patience for people who look for loopholes in my argument – "Why wouldn't you eat a deer? How could you eat an egg?" Yeah, well, we all make judgment calls.

Patrick: Jeremy visits every so often and realizing his Zen-ish eating habits I have to make sure we have something to feed the poor soul. So I came up the "Jeremy Dish". It did not require going out and buying any odd ball stuff I don't usually stock, at least not since my short lived Zen-ish macrobiotic days some 30 years ago. So if you've got one of these plant eaters in your midst you can always pull out this "anti-venom".

Jeremy's Dish

INGREDIENTS: Fresh bell peppers (red, green, yellow) cut into medium sized chunks, potatoes cut into medium size chunks, onion, zucchini, pasta.

- Oil in pan.
- Fry potatoes.
- Add, peppers and onions.
- Then add zucchini.
- Season with salt and pepper.

Serve over rigatoni (my choice) but a fresh pasta will work great as well. Double starch, so what, its good and it keeps him from eating our house plants.

John: Since Jeremy would visit me and his step-mom summers between his college years, we decided not to eat meat because it was basically easier to cook one meal that everyone could eat, regardless of who cooked it. I bought an Indian cookbook which focused on vegetarian dishes from the south of India. It was all new to me – the flavors, the spices, the preparations – so it took some getting used to. But in time we got the hang of it, and this style of food became our mainstay for a while. Eventually Jeremy graduated from college, got a job back East and didn't spend his summers with us any more. I began to miss the texture and flavors of certain meat dishes, so we slowly drifted back to including meat in our diet. I should emphatically add here that while we were not eating meat, both my wife and I felt a whole lot healthier. Our digestive systems, generally somewhat of a problem for both of us, functioned better, and we seemed to have more energy and a brighter disposition. Still we gravitated to meat once again, because we missed it. But we don't eat meat nearly every night. Fish is probably a bigger part of our diet than meat, and many of our meals are vegetarian. Regardless of whether we eat meat, vegetables are a big part of every meal, in addition to salads.

All of this prattle reminds me of a couple of things and a couple of stories. So before we get to the recipes, hear me out. You might enjoy my blathering.

Philosophical Aside

John: As I've said earlier, I've grown accustomed to a Tuscan/Provençal style of cooking and eating, so that's what predominates in this book. But I hesitate to call this an Italian or Provençal cookbook. It's about how to think about getting comfortable in the kitchen. But maybe more than that it's about finding a "cuisine", or a food ethos, or a cooking lifestyle that suits you. That you enjoy and get to know and understand. This book is about gaining some consistency in how you eat, and not bouncing all over the culinary world each day, cooking a faux Mexican recipe out of some magazine one night, and some Creole fritters the next, chop suey the next, and so on. All foods are wonderful, and you should experience and enjoy all the world's variety. Besides Italian and Provençal, I especially enjoy Thai, Indian, Southwestern American, Japanese, Oaxacan. But settle on something that can get to be your "adoptive" style and live with it. My theory is that over the millennia, the peoples of every region in the world adopted the food that was right for them, which was usually what they could raise in their climates and terrains, or catch in their seas and forests. Their bodies over time adjusted to the food, expected the food, and knew what to do with it. Getting close to your food is important I think. You become intimate with it. You fall in love with it. It becomes literally and figuratively what you are about – who you are.

The Chez Panisse Note

One day while I was at work in my office in Berkeley, I decided to call my wife and suggest that we meet at Chez Panisse for dinner, that very evening. Now, for those of you who don't know, Chez Panisse is a world famous restaurant started by Alice Waters in Berkeley, California. It was the beginning of "California" or West Coast cuisine, basically using classical French style cooking but the flavors and ingredients of the new world, especially the new world of the western United States. Alice spawned many of the noted chefs we know today including Wolfgang Puck and Mark Miller, to name but two of many. The restaurant was in an old Berkeley "brown shingle" house, on a busy street, right around the corner from where we lived. And we had never eaten there. Why? Well, it was expensive, it mainly served meat (and the menus were fixed every night – no choices) and this was our "vegetarian" period, and it was typically very hard to get a reservation. For us it was hard to get around all these obstacles, especially the planning ahead part (weeks if not months in advance).

So this afternoon in question, I picked up the phone and called Chez Panisse and announced to the person answering the phone, "I want to come to Chez Panisse tonight with my wife for dinner".

"Well, let me see", said the man, putting me on hold for a few seconds. "It seems we have a cancellation (by the way when you make a reservation here they take your credit card number, and charge you whether you show up of not) for the six thirty seating. Do you want me to reserve the table for you?"

"Sure," I said. "See you then!" I hung up. (After giving him my Amex number, of course).

Uh-oh! I forgot to ask what the meal's courses were. We were vegetarian after all. I dialed the number again.

"Hello, Chez Panisse", the same man answered.

"Yes, I just took the table you offered a few seconds ago, but forgot to ask you what the menu was for this evening", I admitted.

He rattled off a series of wonderful sounding things, and coming to the main entrée said, "And a Harris Ranch beef rib eye steak, grilled, with a butter sauce".

"Yikes", I said. Actually, my wife and I don't eat meat. I should have clarified this before I reserved this table. But we do eat fish."

"Let me ask the chef", he replied calmly, and again placed me on hold. "The chef says he has some very nice wild salmon steaks he can make for you, if you wish," he returned saying.

"Wow! That's super. See you later! Thanks! Bye".

That night as everyone was being served their steaks (the only thing you had to say to the waiter all night was to tell him what wine you wanted, otherwise the service was perfect, well-orchestrated, and on-plan) we got our salmon steaks and watched people look at us like we were maybe celebrities. Who knows what they thought. It was I think our most memorable dining out experience, except for the night in Seattle that I proposed marriage to my wife at "Chez Shea", a classic French restaurant over-looking the Puget Sound.

Now that's how to run a restaurant. The single most famous restaurant, if not in the entire U.S. then definitely on the West Coast, and the least snooty. A smooth, cool group of professionals. You won't find that in NY or LA. Though my favorite restaurant in the United States is Il Cantinori in NYC. Well, I have to add that my co-favorite is Zuni Café in San Francisco.

> 🍽 Note to Portland restaurateurs: Portland, "pound-for-pound", has more pretty darn good restaurants than just about any other city in the States. The food culture here, and my daughter and grandchildren, are what keep me here. And I might add, New Seasons supermarket.

The Alice Waters Note

Remember, Alice started Chez Panisse, trained many of the country's leading cooks, and has become one of America's food icons. One day on the local NPR station she was being interviewed because she had convinced the local Berkeley school board to let her start a vegetable garden in the back of one of the middle schools. The premise was to teach kids about eating more healthfully, by growing, harvesting, and cooking their own vegetables. Now remember, Chez Panisse was all about French cooking updated for the modern California palate (i.e. lots of meat, fat, cream and butter). The conceit was that she wanted kids to abandon the fat in McDonald's burgers and fries for a more healthful diet, when she had, and was, making her fortune selling their parents delicious things slathered with fat. I've never reconciled myself to her little deceit, but she could probably care less, especially since I've never met her and have never made this little diatribe public before.

The Nancy Barrows Note

My wife has had several "hobbies", or obsessions I call them, since I met her fifteen years ago. Some have been dressage, knitting, sewing, and growing award-winning roses. Currently, she gardens, growing bushels of chard, kale, squash, turnips, carrots, beans of various kinds, beets, onions, shallots, apples, tomatoes, potatoes, figs, grapes, kiwis, garlic, raspberries, peas, and many varieties of lettuce greens. Many practically year-round in our temperate Portland climate.

One night she declared, "I like vegetables more than you do".

"Whatever, Dude", was the only trite, stunned reply I could muster.

The Debbie Barrows Note

Patrick: My wife is the vegetable psycho in the household. Our daughter and myself always roll our eyes when she begins to go into her speeches about the beauty of fresh vegetables, especially untouched by any additional seasonings or sauces. And she won't release her verbal "talons" until we take our share. Now don't get me wrong, she is not a vegetarian or vegan or whatever term is used. She will guard the bone from her steak like a wild animal with crazed blood shot eyes, and would sooner pin your hand to the table with her steak knife, like the scene from the Godfather, than have you try to take it. Ya' gotta love her!

Cooking Greens

Basically there are two methods that I employ for cooking all the fresh greens that my wife *forces* on me. These will work for chard, kale, mustard greens, collards, etc.

Method one
- Wash each leaf under cool running water.
- Pull out tough center vein of kale, spinach, collards, etc.
- Chop the leaves very roughly.
- Soak in cold, salted water for a while.
- Life out the leaves in handfuls and transfer to a large skillet-type pan that has a cover, allowing some of the water to cling to the leaves.
- Turn on the heat and cover the pan.
- Steam the greens lightly in the small amount of water, adding a little water if necessary. You might also add some chopped garlic to the pan before steaming.
- Remove cover, add some salt and pepper and simmer away most of the remaining liquid.
- Turn off heat and drizzle some olive oil over the greens, and maybe a drop of Balsamic or lemon juice, too before serving.

My wife actually does this much better than me, which I can't figure out. But she's the vegetable lover, after all. Her technique I think is to ignore, or forget about, them once she's started the cooking. Sometime they run out of cooking liquid and scorch a little, adding a unique, but not undelightful flavor.

> 🍽 *You may instead prepare a little pureed garlic, lemon juice, salt, oil, vinegar vinaigrette to drizzle on the cooked greens. You might also add some lightly toasted pignoli.*

My wife also likes to add some chopped preserved lemon sometimes to the greens after cooking. Preserved lemon is the rind of whole lemons pickled in lemon juice, water, and spices. Meyer lemons work best.

Method Two
- Boil ("blanche", actually) the greens in lots of salted water. This only takes a few seconds, depending on the vegetable.
- Drain completely and plunge into cold water to stop the cooking, and drain again.
- Dry in paper towels and chop to a consistency that pleases you.
- Sautee some garlic in some oil, and add the greens.
- Heat and stir.
- Salt and pepper.
- Maybe some lemon juice. Maybe some pine nuts.

About these greens recipes, in general. If your spouse, children, or significant other(s) will allow it, chop up some pancetta or salt pork and sauté under well-rendered in the olive oil before sautéing the greens. The pork fat flavor and the sweet, crunchy pork "croutons" are a delight.

> 🍴 *Blanching is the act of dumping vegetables into lots of salted water, to start the cooking of them, which is completed in a later stage such as sautéing. The blanching should not thoroughly cook the vegetable, still leaving it crunchy but not raw tasting. This should only take a minute, more or less. In every case, immediately drain and plunge into very cold water to stop the cooking, which helps keep the vegetable's bright, fresh green color intact, then drain and dry.*

Potatoes

John: Relax. I'm not going to tell you how to boil, mash, or bake. Here are some ideas other than that.

Patrick: You might as well "unrelax" now because I *am* going to talk about, boiling, mashing and baking. The reason being is I am assuming there will be *some* people reading this book who have little or no experience in the kitchen whether they be newlyweds or singles. Even the most basic of basics must be touched upon. So while "Mr. High Falootin'" might abandon you, I won't.

Mashed Potatoes

INGREDIENTS: Figure one medium size potato per person, olive oil or butter, milk, salt and pepper.

- Peel the potatoes and put in a big enough pot and cover with water.
- Bring to a boil and let cook until the tines of a 2 prong fork pierce them fairly easily.
- Be careful not to over cook.
- Drain the water.
- Add some milk, a little at a time.
- Begin mashing with a hand masher.
- Add maybe a tbsp of butter or olive oil and a few shakes of salt and pepper.
- Mash some more.
- If too dry, add some more milk a little at a time until you have achieved a firm but soft texture. Too much milk will turn the potatoes into thick soup so you must pay attention and add a little at a time, mashing in between.

You may want to add some fresh minced chives or garlic to the potatoes.

Baked Potatoes

INGREDIENTS: One russet potato per person

- Wash the potatoes but do not peel them.
- Pierce the skins with a fork in a few spots. This will allow steam to escape and prevent the potato from exploding.
- Bake on the center rack at 350 degrees for about an hour. Use a fork to test doneness. They should be easily pierced without hardly any resistance.

Good with many different things to put on top such as sour cream, butter, salt & pepper etc. Eat the skins. They are good and full of vitamins.

Boiled Potatoes

INGREDIENTS: One potato per person. Do not use baking potatoes because they turn too "floury" when boiled.

- Peel the potatoes and boil as you did for mashed potatoes.
- The only difference is you are not going to mash these.
- When done, (and do *not* over cook) drain and serve.

Typically served as a St. Patrick's Day side, with corned beef and cabbage.

Fried Potatoes with Onions

INGREDIENTS: One potato per person, one onion per person, olive oil, butter, salt & pepper.

- Put some butter and olive oil in a good size heavy frying pan and heat. Peel the onions and slice them super thin and add to the pan.
- Sauté for a few minutes.
- Peel the potatoes and either slice or cube them. Add them to the pan.
- Add Salt & pepper.
- Stir and toss with a spatula.
- Lower heat and let slow cook uncovered until browned and tender making sure to toss and flip them on a regular basis so they all cook evenly.

French Fries

John: OK, OK. I told you to forget frying at home. But for those of you who won't listen:

- Cut raw peeled potatoes into thick slices or French fry shapes. At this point I'd soak them in cold water for a while, drain and dry them.
- Put only one layer of potatoes on the bottom of a large heavy skillet. Doesn't matter if you crowd them, but just one layer.
- Pour in enough fresh corn, peanut, or canola to just barely cover the potatoes.
- Put the pan on the stove and turn on the heat.
- As the oil heats it will begin to bubble and sizzle
- Continue cooking until the potatoes are brown and crisp.
- Turn off the heat.
- Lift out the potatoes with a slotted spoon and drain on paper towels.
- Salt and serve.

No kidding!

Try with sweet potatoes, too. Shoot, I've never done it, but maybe try turnips or parsnips, or jicama, or daikon, or carrots.

Patrick: Well he blew me away with this technique. I would never think of starting with cold potatoes and cold oil like that. The tendency, I found was that the potatoes would absorb much more oil if it was not brought up to high temperature first. Then I use a double fry method.

John: Well, they don't absorb the oil when cold. As it turns out, the reason why "French fries" are double-cooked, is that in restaurants it is quicker to half pre-cook them. Then when an order comes in, they're finished with a final dip into the hot fat.

Patrick: That may be true for the more upscale restaurants that make their own fries. But the bulk of restaurants buy pre-cut, pre-cooked bags of frozen fries and just throw them into the oil. The double fry method creates the crispness. When the potatoes are cooked the first time the oil heat drops when they are added and essentially cooking them in boiling oil. They are then removed and the oil is then brought to a higher temperature which when the potatoes are returned will quickly *crisped* on the outside and then quickly removed.

Roasted Potatoes

- Take baking potatoes and quarter them lengthwise, without peeling.
- Soak them in lots of cold water to rid of excess starch.
- Drain, rinse, and dry.
- Put into a bowl with olive oil and fresh chopped rosemary or sage.
- Mix well.
- Place them skin side down on foil lined cookie sheets (with edges).
- Drizzle the olive oil/herb mixture over.
- Salt lightly.
- Put in a hot oven and roast until very brown, crusty, and puffy.
- Salt some more and serve.

I like to dip in Dijon mustard or a hot sauce and eat.

Potato Salad

INGREDIENTS: Boiling potatoes, white wine vinegar, yellow prepared mustard, spicy prepared mustard, sugar, mayonnaise, radishes, scallions, hard-boiled eggs.

- Boil potatoes whole, in their skins.
- Drain and cool in a bowl in the refrigerator.
- When cool peel them and cut into small cubes.
- Hard boil and cool some eggs.
- Make a dressing of white wine vinegar, salt, pepper, sugar, Dijon mustard, mustard, mayonnaise.
- Chop some radishes and scallions and add to the potatoes.
- Peel and slice the eggs and add.
- Pour over the dressing and mix.

This is usually served chilled

Patrick: That recipe was a dish we grew up eating, but of course I modified, and it looks like John did too. I use cider vinegar for one. I also add honey, instead of sugar, to balance the vinegar. The use of fresh chives is also my preference over scallions. On occasion, I will mash up one of the eggs and add to the dressing to really spread the flavor around. An important note here is to make sure the potatoes are cold. If you add dressing to warm potatoes, they will absorb the dressing and leave the dish "dry". You want a semi-creamy salad so the dressing consistency should be somewhat thinner than say ketchup.

Something Like Julia's Potato Salad

John: Unlike Pat's remonstration that one should not add dressing to warm potatoes, in this recipe adding some liquid to the still warm potatoes adds flavor by allowing the warmth to absorb the liquid. The dressing is added later.

INGREDIENTS: Boiling potatoes, broth, dry vermouth, a basic vinaigrette (i.e. garlic, salt, lemon juice, vinegar, olive oil, pepper, and a little Dijon), fresh herbs of your choice (chives, parsley, thyme, lavender, etc.).

- Boil potatoes whole.
- Drain and when cooled just enough to handle, peel, quarter and slice into about an eighth inch thickness.
- Put them in a bowl and splash some dry white vermouth and some chicken stock over them, mixing lightly and letting sit so that they absorb the liquids.
- Make a vinaigrette.
- At this point I chop up some herbs.
- Add the herbs and mix in the vinaigrette.
- Fresh pepper and salt.

This is best served just slightly warm from the still warm potatoes, or at room temp.

Tomatoes

They must be fresh homegrown (or market purchased) heirlooms. Pick your own favorite flavor, and make sure they're ripe.

"Nude-ish"

- Slice thickly and place on a large plate in one layer
- Sprinkle with salt
- Chiffonnade some fresh basil and sprinkle over the tomatoes.
- Drizzle with good olive oil
- Grind some fresh pepper.

Maybe add some very fresh, hand made mozzarella slices sitting on top of each tomato slice.

Patrick: I wish I knew what "chiffonnade" meant, then I might be able to do it. Probably just another frilly "apron-boy" term that means "torn into small pieces."

John: Not quite. But if you weren't so "prol" you would know.

Patrick: I am beginning to see what I missed by not going to finishing school like John, but I have no regrets.

With Roasted Peppers (Peperonata)

INGREDIENTS: Red and/or yellow bell peppers, tomatoes, onion, red wine vinegar.

- Roast, peel and slice the peppers into strips.
- Sauté some sliced onions.
- Add the peppers and sauté.
- Add some chopped fresh tomatoes and simmer.
- Add a dab of red wine vinegar.
- Salt and pepper.
- Simmer and stir until slightly thickened and a little amalgamated.

You may want to add some capers and/or slices from un-pitted olives. Maybe add a hot chili pepper, chopped, to the pan while cooking. Serve warm, or at room temp, but not hot, letting the flavors meld a little.

> 🍽 **Roasting peppers note:** *Take red, yellow, or orange bell peppers and roast them over an open flame on your gas range. Alternatively roast them under your oven's broiler, turning periodically until the entire pepper is blackened and charred. With tongs, pop them into a plastic bag and let them steam and rest. One at a time take a pepper and rub off the skins with your fingers under cool running water. Remove the stems and seeds and cut pepper into thin long strips.*

Eggplant, Zucchini, Onions

"Napoleons"

John: This can be a layered dish using one, two, or all of the above.

INGREDIENTS: Eggplant and/or zucchini, parsley, olive oil, vinaigrette, cumin (optional).

- Trim and slice the eggplant and/or zucchini in half lengthwise.
- Laying the cut side down on the cutting board, run a very sharp knife along the bottom side of the eggplant cutting a very thin slice. Hold the eggplant down with the palm of your other hand.
- Continue slicing the rest of the eggplant/zucchini into slices.
- Heat a stove top grill very, very hot (a ridged grill preferable).
- Dry roast the slices until they're well browned, and even slightly charred, but not over-cooked or totally dried out, a few at a time. Turn once to do both sides.
- Lay on paper towels as cooked.
- Make a layered dish, alternating the vegetable layers with parsley, a vinaigrette (maybe flavored with some cumin) and extra olive oil.
- Let marinate for a while.
- Serve at room temp.

Sautéed
INGREDIENTS: Eggplant and/or zucchini, garlic, olive oil, lemon juice, parsley.

- Cube eggplant or zucchini.
- Sautee in olive oil and garlic, browning all sides well, but do not mush up.
- Maybe dribble on some lemon juice.
- Sprinkle with some parsley.

> 🍽 **Note:** *I like the smaller eggplant varieties and small zucchini. I especially like white eggplant. The best zucchini are Romanesco, which you never find in a store. You'll have to find them in a good seed catalog and grow them yourself. They have well defined ridges running lengthwise along them. They stay crunchier during cooking, and have a nutlike flavor.*

Onions

John: I don't waste my money on onions that are "sweet", or red, or white, or small or large, or whatever the marketing gimmick is. I buy the cheapest, make sure each one I select is firm and has no rotting spots or bruises. Unless you want to eat the onion raw, like an apple, you don't need Walla Wallas or Vidalias. "Sweetness" simply means that they have a lower concentration of a sulfuric-type acid in them than regular onions. That's the stuff that burns your eyes when you chop them (and blinded the poor phantom of the opera). Instead you can cut the onion in two and soak it in cold water for a while to leach out and dilute the acid, if you want to avoid crying while you chop, or if you want to use the onion raw in a salad or something. Or you simply "sweat" the chopped onion in some butter or oil if you're using them in a cooked dish, before you add the other ingredients. You're just literally sweating out the acid and whatever excess moisture you don't want in the dish. Getting rid of the acid inherently makes the onion sweeter.

Patrick: I think you lost it, mon! If you don't notice the difference in taste between the various onion varieties then go directly to jail, do not pass go and do not collect $200. I use specific onions for specific purposes, which I will not go into here, but which you will see in recipes.

John: Patrick also uses pink peppercorns, blue Caspian Sea salt, and red carrots. Some people are much more creative than I'll ever be.

Creamed Onions

Patrick: This is a recipe I only make at Christmas time. It does not use your typical white sauce and tastes nothing like what you are probably accustomed to.

INGREDIENTS: Fresh pearl onions, butter, sugar, heavy cream, minced fresh parsley, salt.

- Blanch the onions in hot water then drain and put in a bowl of cold water.
- Remove the root ends and the outer skin.
- Put them in a heavy pot with the butter, sugar and salt.
- Add just enough water to cover.
- Put on high heat and let boil, uncovered until the all the water evaporates.
- Continually stir the onions as they will now begin to caramelize.
- They will start to brown and the bottom of the pan will begin to brown.
- When nice and lightly browned, remove from heat and add the heavy cream and parsley. Return to medium heat and reduce to a thickish consistency which will turn light brown from the caramelizing.
- Transfer to a serving bowl.

Asparagus

John: I like the very thin kind.

- Wash the spears and snap off the white, pulpy ends with your hands. They'll break in the right spot.
- Put in a sauté pan that has a top, with a little water and some oil and/or butter.
- Put on the top and steam until still crunchy.
- Remove top and continue to sauté until the liquid is gone and the spears brown or even char a little.

Serve with some lemon juice, oil, salt and pepper. Or maybe a fresh made aioli or rouille.

Patrick: Asparagus is a biggie around our house with the wife and daughter. Their preference is to grill (i.e. blacken) them on a hot cast iron stove top pan. Salt & pepper, oil and lemon.

Green Beans

Sautéed
John: I like the thin, French style varieties for this. Fresh Romano beans are great, too.

I cook them in pretty much the same way as the asparagus, except you might try grating some Parmigiano on them when serving
Sometimes after I finish sautéing the asparagus or beans, especially in butter, I might deglaze the pan with a little dry vermouth until I have a nice reduction and pour that over the vegetable.

Carrots and Parsnips

Sorry, I'm not a huge carrot fan. Though I don't dislike them by any means. But if you cook them like I like to cook parsnips, they're OK.

- Clean, scrape and slice the parsnips.
- Par boil (blanche) and drain.
- Sautee in butter
- Add salt and lots of pepper.

Maybe sprinkle with some thyme or parsley. Maybe add some honey drizzled on.

 Carrots, especially in soups, also work well with fresh ginger as an accompanying flavor.

Beets

Buy them at the market with the root end and greens still attached. Before cooking cut off the greens (you can cook the greens separately if you want, if they're not too tough, ratty looking, or old) but leaving an inch or two of green attached as this helps keep the beets' deep color from leaching out during boiling.

You can boil, steam, or roast (enclosed in foil) the beets, but I prefer boiling. It's easier to check doneness.

- Boil the beets in salted water, checking them once or twice with a wood skewer to see when they're done. Don't let them get over-cooked.
- Drain and add cold water to pan, letting the beets cool down completely.
- Under cool running water, rub the skins off. The root end and remaining stem will rub off easily as well.
- I then usually quarter and slice them (on a piece of wax paper to avoid staining my cutting board too much).
- Put the slices into a bowl and use for a recipe right away or store in the fridge until you're ready to use them.

I Think These Are Called "Harvard Beets" (at least my rendition)

INGREDIENTS: Cooked and peeled beets, butter, vinegar, flour or cornstarch, sugar.

- Sauté the sliced beets in butter until warmed up.
- Add a little vinegar.
- Add a little sugar.
- Stir.
- Sprinkle on a little flour or cornstarch, and stir.
- Add a little water to thicken slightly and create a sauce.
- Salt and pepper.

Chilled Beet "Salad"

- Make a vinaigrette, with some herbs if you like.
- Pour over the sliced, cooled or room temp beets and toss lightly.

Options:
- Add some crumbled goat cheese.
- Add some lightly toasted nuts such as walnuts.

Turnips/Rutabagas

I do like these because they were a staple of Uncle Claude's and Aunt Rose's root cellar, and they are very traditional "Yankee" fare. Nevertheless, my wife had to remind me to add them.

- Peel and cut into chunks.
- Boil in salted water until done.
- Drain.
- Mash and/or whip with lots of butter, salt, and pepper and some milk and/or cream.

They should be creamy. Add butter and more pepper to serve. Sometimes it's nice to blend with mashed potatoes. It helps both the potato and the turnip - vegetable synergy I guess.

Braised Turnips with Duck Legs

I've also invented a braised duck leg recipe in which peeled, thickly sliced slabs of big rutabagas are slowly braised in the braising liquid.

INGREDIENTS: Duck legs, turnips, herbs, red wine.

- In a heavy Dutch oven, brown, then slowly sauté duck legs, skin side down, in their own fat for a while until the legs age very crispy and most of the fat is rendered.
- Remove most of the rendered fat, and add red wine, and herbs (a bundle say of bay, garlic, celery leaves, thyme branches, shallot, etc.).
- Cover and braise on the stove top or in a slowish oven until legs are very, very tender.
- Remove cover and duck legs, add the peeled and very thickly sliced turnips to the liquid, and cook them while the liquid reduces.
- I like to run the duck legs under a broiler (or just stick them back in the hot oven) to crisp them up a little.

Serve the legs, the turnips, and reduction together.

John: Cooking vegetables isn't hard. The gist of it is, keep it simple, don't over cook, don't over sauce. Don't annihilate the subtle beauty of the fresh vegetables' flavors.

Patrick: Well, I am no big fan of vegetables. Never was and never will be. Which reminds me, I am due for a colonoscopy! At any rate, my wife is a vegetable freak and has low cholesterol and a clean colon to show for it. To her, vegetables are best raw or steamed with maybe, and that's a big maybe, a little pepper and olive oil. She enjoys the "true" flavor. She makes me eat vegetables. My preference is grilled!

Grilled Mixed Vegetables

Quantities will vary depending on the number of people to be fed. You may (obviously) mix and match your preferred vegetables but keep in mind some will require less cooking than and therefore their addition to the grill pan is all about timing.
My typical medley is:

- Fresh green and red bell peppers, quartered.
- Vidalia onions sliced thick.
- Fresh whole mushrooms.
- Zucchini cleaned but unpeeled, cut into thick slices .
- Balsamic vinegar.
- Olive oil.
- Salt & pepper.
- Put all the ingredients in a large bowl.
- Sprinkle with vinegar, oil and salt and pepper then mix.
- When grill tray is hot, put vegetables in and grill, flipping occasionally.

The softer vegetables will be added later during the grilling as they will take less time.

Grilled Corn on the Cob

INGREDIENT: The freshest corn you can find.

This is my version of grilled corn which is much easier and cleaner than your usual "in husk" methods.

- Husk the corn and boil in water for about 7-10 minutes.
- Drain on plate.
- Place on hot grill turning very frequently until they start to brown and caramelize.
- Be very watchful and do not over grill or they will dry and wither.

Grilled Potatoes

- Usually I partially the potatoes before grilling.
- Do not peel the potatoes but remove any obvious "issues".
- You can microwave them until they are medium firm or bake them until they are the same.
- Then slice them in half length wise, brush with oil, and sprinkle with salt & pepper.
- Place on hot grill turning as necessary until they are golden brown on both sides.

Provençal Baked Winter Squash

John: Madeleine Vedel (she's actually American, but probably figured she should live in France with Erick and raise a family in Arles, since she has the perfect French first name) told me that she invented and forced this recipe into their cooking school book (since Erick hates squash).

Of course, just splitting a nice winter squash in two, seeding and baking it, and then just melting a little butter in the cavity with salt and pepper , is one of the most simple ways to enjoy this vegetable. And that's what most of us do. Here's a little different idea, that is slightly more "complicated", but always a major hit.

INGREDIENTS: A Winter squash, pancetta, onion, bay leaves, garlic, nutmeg, honey.

- Cut up a winter squash into bit size chucks. No need to peel.
- Saute some chopped up pancetta and onion in olive oil, in a heavy oven-proof casserole or Dutch oven.
- Add squash and lightly brown for a while.
- Add bay, nutmeg, chopped garlic, salt and pepper and stir.
- Drizzle honey all over, but don't stir it in.
- Put in a hot oven until it becomes tender, browns, and the honey caramelizes.

Eggs

John: As I've said before, there was a time in my life that I may have considered beer the perfect food – not that I drank that much of it – but because it seemed so elemental: grain, yeast, water, and even a little herb (hops) flavoring. Not far from the original Etruscan grain mush that sustained them until it evolved into cornmeal polenta, and then into pasta in its various incarnations. But then, and now, with the possible exception of beans, I'd have to name the egg as the closest to a perfect food as there is. You can probably name as many attributes that it has as I can, and as many recipes as they appear in, even if you don't agree with my nomination. So I won't go into that. But at the very least, I think the egg deserves its own lesson, brief and simple as it might be. Like everything else in the food world, I stress quality of the raw material. I think with eggs is most important. Though I tended to buy "cage free", "vegetarian" eggs in my market, which cost about twice as much as the manufactured variety, frankly there isn't that much of a *noticeable* difference in the quality of the egg. Then one day my wife arrived home from work with three baby chicks. Un-forewarned, I had to immediately set to work building a secure coup to house them so they wouldn't fall prey to marauding hawks by day, and hungry raccoons by night. The chickens grew in our fenced yard, eating bugs and grubs, grass, lettuce, while roto-tilling our garden with their incessant scratching and pecking. They were a joy to behold and hysterical to observe. They put themselves to bed at dusk. All I had to do was secure the henhouse door. In the meantime, they gave us the best eggs I've ever recalled eating. The yolks were so deeply yellow they were almost orange. And they were so firm that when they were broken into a skillet to fry, the yolks stood up round and plump, refusing to cave in to gravity. The taste was rich and almost decadent. Eventually the hens aged and ceased prime egg production, and we moved to a less secure chicken environment. So we put them up for adoption to a couple of young girls, whose parents I think preferred chickens as pets to dogs or cats. The moral of the story is, raise your own chickens, if you can. Otherwise, everything else in the egg category is just second best.

The Omelet – according to Julia Child

I think the funniest Julia Child show I ever watched was her omelet show. Though she commanded much more of my esteem when I was younger, than she does now when I watch her shows (that's probably because she really over-did the cream and butter thing) her simple approach to the omelet and her respect for a quality egg remains as a citadel for my culinary imaginings.

> 🍽 Here is as good time as any, as I begin the winding down of my cookbook writing exploit, to talk about the words "culinary", "gourmet", "cuisine" and the like, which hold neither a high-falootin' nor a pejorative meaning in and of themselves. Speaking for myself, and I think I speak for many of you as well, these words can scare, frighten, turn off, intimidate, or confuse many people who don't cook, or those who are not confident enough to embark on their own cooking creativity, simply in the inferences people draw from hearing them spoken. I have gravitated to a style of cooking that I consider simple, clean, healthful in its moderation and balance, and approachable. You may say it's Italian, or Tuscan, or some version of Mediterranean. (And by the way I love just about all of the world's cooking styles that I've encountered). But it's what I like and what I have come to understand enough to actually be confident enough in to enjoy doing. So, if I hear someone say I'm a gourmet cook, I cringe and recoil. I know they're trying to be complimentary, so no shame on them. But I know I'm not a gourmet cook, in the sense that most aficionados of good food would define it. I don't even consider myself a very good cook. It's just that I enjoy cooking and learning about cooking. And I enjoy eating. Take away the challenge of having to become a "better cook", or a gourmet cook, or an excellent cook, or a crowd pleasing cook and you simply realize all you have to do is enjoy it.

Anyway, Julia introduced the omelet show by showing all the kinds of pans invented by various people and companies to help make the perfect omelet – at least by their definition. And as she described the inappropriateness of each pan she disdainfully tossed it over her shoulder, and you could hear it crash onto the floor below or behind her. Then she dragged out her little non-stick (looked like Teflon) rounded edge pan and held it up and said, "Now *that's* an omelet pan!" First she threw a scoop of butter into the hot non-stick pan. She then broke an egg or two into a small bowl, added a drizzle of water, some salt and pepper. She beat the eggs with a fork for a few seconds, waited for the butter's foam to subside (but before it colored), dumped the eggs in and began to swirl and shake the pan to and fro. After about 30 seconds of shaking started back and forth, gravity had forced the now setting eggs toward the back of the pan, whereupon she flipped the back half of the egg mixture over on top of the bottom half, and then turned the omelet onto a plate with the folded side of the omelet down. The whole process maybe took a minute. She then explained how you could add a little chopped ham or cheese or herbs to this quick process, if you wanted to. But even as I write this I picture the typical American "diner" omelet: "Our Famous 6 egg omelet stuffed with 3 cheeses, a pound of ham, a rasher of bacon, roasted jalapeños, creamed spinach, home fried potatoes, and a sweet Italian sausage". You can also get a side of pancakes or a pillbox hat sized buttermilk muffin, and maybe some French fries. I can't order an omelet in a diner because a.) I know that the eggs are low-grade, produced by antibiotic saturated hens b.) Omelets should be about the egg, not the "sauce" (like pasta), and c.) Only "certain un-named people" could eat that much, pay $6.95 and declare "They serve really good portions in that place".

The Frittata – my version
(with my wife's balsamic reduction)

INGREDIENTS: Eggs, balsamic vinegar, onions.

- Preheat the oven.
- Separate eggs.
- Add a little water to the yolks and stir with a fork.
- Beat the egg whites until just beginning to stiffen.
- Simmer balsamic vinegar until it's syrupy.
- Sauté some sliced onions in some butter and olive oil until caramelized in a normal sized stainless steel sauté pan with rounded sides.
- Fold the whites into the yolks and pour unto the hot skillet.
- Swirl around a little to set the edges, then pop into the oven to finish.
- Flip it over onto a serving dish if you feel like taking the risk.
- Serve with the balsamic reduction .

You may want to add some crumbled goat cheese before you bake. The frittata will be light and fluffy.

Poached egg – with baguette

- Poach an egg or two by breaking into simmering water that has a touch of vinegar. I like to keep the yolk runny, but past the watery stage.
- Lift out with a slotted spoon and place on a long horizontal slice of buttered baguette toast.
- Serve with some jam on the side.

Fried – my favorite

- Fry sunny side up.
- Serve with corned beef hash.
- Add Mexican hot sauce.

Hard-boiled

- Simmer slowly for long enough to cook them.
- Immediately drain and add cold water to the pot.
- Drain and put eggs into fridge to completely cool.
- Peel and eat with salt.

Sorry, I'm *really* not trying to insult you here, but it's about the egg. It is nature's very own perfect food, after all.

As I conclude this chapter, I am recalling the very last scene in one of my favorite films of all time, "Big Night". It's about two Italian immigrant brothers in 1950's New Jersey, who open a small authentic Italian restaurant. It's a movie you must see, even if you aren't a cook, or a "foodie". To summarize, the brothers struggle to survive, mainly because Primo, the older brother and the chef (being a typical "chef") refuses to compromise his standards and adjust to the Americanized version of Italian food. The younger brother, Secondo, is the go-getter and wants very much to be successful, in the American way. The tension between the two is the crux of the movie, and the tension eventually breaks them apart, sending Primo back to Rome to work in his uncle's restaurant. In the final scene, in which we assume will be the brothers' final meal together they are sitting in the very wee hours of the morning in the kitchen after an exhausting, yet very unfulfilling night in the restaurant replete with an incredible array of complex dishes (I won't spoil it for you here, since the night is the point of the whole story. Secondo, without any words being spoken, breaks two eggs into a bowl and stirs them, while heating some olive oil in a skillet. He turns the beaten eggs into the skillet, swirls them gently, then divides and slides them onto two white plates. He breaks two pieces of bread from a loaf and places one on each plate. Silently they eat their final meal together.

Patrick: Well, I got news for you, as my wife tells it and researched it, honey is the perfect food, not eggs.

And while I'm at it I'll tell you the real way to make a frittata. Not the "beginner's", I mean "Master's", way.

Well if you want to do it the beginner's way above, that's fine. If not then listen up: There is no oven needed.

- You fold the onions into the egg mixture once they have cooled slightly. By the way, you can forgo the beaten egg whites and just beat the eggs as one. If cooked properly, they will turn out just as light anyway. But if you want to be cute, Like Johnny, then by all means do the beaten egg white thing.
- Use a clean sauté pan to which you have added some olive oil and heat.
- Once heated pour your egg mixture in it.
- Lift the edges so the uncooked eggs on top can drain onto the pan below.
- When most of the wetness of the top is done then put a plate on top of the sauté pan and flip the pan over onto the plate then slide back into the pan.
- Finishing cooking on that side.

Serve on a platter and the balsamic sauce reduction above.

Green Beans and Eggs

This is a variation of a Tuscan recipe which uses asparagus and fried eggs. Although that recipe was good, I found a need to play with it and create something for a cold winters evening or even breakfast for that matter. This is a spicy, peppery dish.

INGREDIENTS: Fresh green beans, cut into shorter lengths and soaked in cold water, eggs, olive oil, minced pancetta, red pepper flakes, whole cloves, garlic, water, vinegar, salt, fresh ground black pepper, good artisan bread for toasting.

- Put garlic oil, and garlic in sauté pan with minced pancetta and red pepper flakes.
- Sauté until pancetta begins to cook off its fat and garlic is lightly browned.
- Add the drained beans and mix.
- Sauté this mixture, adding just a little water to create some steam, and cover.
- Stir every so often making sure the mixture is not frying and still creating a little steam.
- Get a skillet of water simmering with a little red wine vinegar in it.
- When the beans have become tender, remove the top and let any water left inside evaporate.
- Carefully add the eggs to the simmering water water. Do not break the yolks.
- You want the eggs to be very yolky but not have watery whites.
- Remove each egg to a large serving bowl and chop up with a knife and fork. It will be very yolky and "soupy".
- Now add the bean mixture and mix it all together.
- Add freshly ground pepper to make the mixture very peppery , a pinch of salt and stir again.
- Serve over an individual good artisan bread toast slices.

John: Is that akin to "Green Eggs and Ham"?

Patrick: Pay no attention to him.

Egg and....On A Roll

Where I live you can pretty much walk into any joint that has a grill and order a "bacon, egg and cheese on a roll". No questions asked, it's just done and you're on your way. I have not had this same experience in other parts of the country, unfortunately, and I'd have to explain or settle for something I consider stupid or sissified. Basically, you start with a fried egg. Cook it the way you like it, but here is what I do: Put a little olive oil in a skillet. Heat it up and crack the egg into the pan. Fry on medium heat until the white begins to turn white then flip it. After about a minute flip the egg back over onto the top of a couple slices of ham that you've thrown into the pan. Put a slice of Swiss or white American on top and cover with a top of a pan that has enough height not to touch the egg below it. When the cheese is melted, take the egg combo off the grill and put on a hard roll. If you don't know what a hard roll is then just put it on toast or a hamburger style roll if that's all you have. If you are cooking the egg over easy you will want to puncture the yolk at this point to let it run and let the bread soak it up so it doesn't "pop" when you bite into it and get all over the place. Now, if you like bacon I suggest you cook a whole pound of it and keep it stored in the refrigerator a few days or longer in the freezer. To cook bacon that is effortless and it comes out flat and crisp, just lay the strips out in a baking sheet with edges and bake until done. No need to flip. Drain on paper towels. When you are ready to make a bacon, egg and cheese, all you have to do is nuke a few slices of the precooked bacon for a few seconds and put them on top of the eggs before adding the cheese. A whole lot better than serving up yourself, your kids or your spouse some pre-made processed crud from the grocer's freezer.

|◉| Note: *I have a story that tells of how passion over expectations wins when cooking, in an old story written back in 1952 called, "The Secret Ingredient". There once was a great cook in a little out of the way town in France. He very much wanted to be upgraded from the 3 crossed spoons and forks to adding much regarded stars by the Michelin Guide. One day he got a letter from an anonymous diner from the past that a representative from Michelin would be visiting him on a certain day. The day he got the letter was the day the tester was to arrive. Shortly a glittery car pulled up to his restaurant and a stout man exited. At once a flurry of activity took place in the kitchen to prepare a dish that would certainly bring him his precious stars, "le Homard dans la Lune" (Lobster in the Moon), an exacting and tricky dish. Well, everything that could go wrong indeed went wrong. When the dish was brought to the diner, the man burst out in disgust after one bite, stormed out announcing that he would see to it that the restaurant would be finished when he got done with him and he left. Highly discouraged and irate, the great cook hauled off and kicked his beloved cat in the butt and out the door, for which he felt great remorse later. After no luck in locating the cat he decided to make the cat his very own "Poularde Surprise Royale" to lure him back home He proclaimed, "I will cook this for you like I have never done before!" Instantly he and his assistants had the kitchen humming with efficiency and passion. Shortly after it was done a traveler showed up at the door. The cook's wife let him in and set him at the table and served him some of the "Poularde Surprise Royale". With one bite, the diner exclaimed, "not in thirty years as a Michelin inspector have I eaten such an exquisite "Poularde Surprise Royale!" I recognize all the ingredients but one. You must tell me what it is!" The great chef declared that he could not disclose the secret ingredient and the diner understood saying, "I shall have two stars added to your restaurant!" The chef had created his Michelin-starred dish with passion, but without the stress and worry. The secret, loving, ingredient he had added to his dear cat's very own "Poulard Surpise Royale" was catnip.*

John: I thought he had added the cat!

Salads

John: Another brief, but important lesson. So short in fact that when this show hits the "Food Network", it'll probably have to be combined with something else, like the Egg lesson, for example.

As with any category, there are as many salads as anyone can dream up. Here are two. One I use every night, and the other when I can get fresh albacore tuna.

First a salad note.

> **Note:** *In many places that I've been in Europe, people tend to eat a salad at or near the end of a meal. So, that's what I started to do some time ago. Sometimes when I do that with people I haven't shared a meal with before, I think that they get the feeling that I'm trying to be, well, "European". I do it because, it helps my digestion. Eating it last, I hypothesize, moves things along, as it were. Then, there's the cleansing the palate factor. If you have a clean salad dressed with oil and vinegar, the freshest and slight bitterness helps scour the palate of sauces, greases, and any lingering aftertastes that you don't want to take to the dessert or cheese course – or to the couch to watch a film. Of course, then there's the fact that I just like the taste and the healthful green leafy aspects. So I eat a simple salad at the end of every meal, and I strongly recommend that you do to.*

Salad

- I buy fresh green lettuces in the market like red leaf, green leaf, romaine, escarole, endive, mixed baby greens, and my wife also raises lettuces just about year round.

- About an hour before dinner time, I wash each leaf, one at a time, under cold running water, flap it dry, tearing it apart if necessary in more bite sized pieces, and place it in a bowl lined with paper towels. I then fold over the outer edges of the towels to completely cover and enclose the leaves. I put the bowl into the fridge until the end of the meal.

- When ready to serve the salad, take the leaves out of the bowl still wrapped in the paper towels. Put a very little balsamic vinegar (or any vinegar, or lemon juice, or a combination) in the bowl. Grind in some fresh salt and pepper, and whisk around to dissolve. Drizzle in olive oil, about 4 – 5 times as the amount of vinegar, while whisking into a blended suspension. Empty the leaves from the towels into the bowl and toss.

A Salad Nicoise – my rendition

INGREDIENTS: Fresh tuna (canned if you must), herbs, boiling potatoes, dry vermouth, hard-boiled eggs, vinaigrette, green beans, anchovy fillets, fresh ripe tomatoes, lettuce, un-pitted olive, capers.

- If I can find some good fresh tuna in the market (I like albacore), I braise it for quite a while in wine, a little broth, and herbs in a heavy covered pot, in the oven or over a slow flame. This can be done anytime, even several days before assembling the salad, but at least long enough before to cool the tuna after it's cooked. After cooling I chunk it apart with my fingers.
- Boil some quartered red or yellow potatoes, though not baking potatoes, skinning them before or after they cook. When cool enough to handle, but still warm, slice the quarters into slices and put in a bowl. Sprinkle some broth and some dry white vermouth over the slices, then lightly toss them so that the potatoes absorb the liquid.
- Boil some eggs hard and cool them. Then quarter or slice them.
- Make a vinaigrette with some lemon juice, pureed garlic, white wine vinegar, salt and pepper, mustard, and olive oil.
- Trim some green beans, throw them into a lot of boiling water for a couple of minutes, then immediately drain and plunge into cold water. When cool, drain them and let dry in a towel.
- Prepare some anchovy fillets, either from a can or those packed in salt.
- Quarter or slice some ripe tomatoes.
- Wash, dry and chill some lettuce leaves, leaving them whole.
- Make a bed of the lettuce in a large shallow bowl, or platter, and drizzle some vinaigrette on.
- Add the potatoes and beans, and drizzle some more vinaigrette.
- Add the anchovies, tuna, and tomatoes and drizzle the rest of the vinaigrette.
- Sprinkle on chopped herbs to suit your taste. Parsley, basil, thyme, lavender, oregano, etc.
- Add some un-pitted olives, and some capers if you wish.

Serve without tossing. Salt and pepper each serving as each person desires.

Caesar's Salad

Caesar Salad is not an Italian recipe – from anywhere in Italy, that is. It was invented by an Italian named Caesar, at his restaurant in Tijuana, Mexico.

INGREDIENTS: Romaine, garlic, lemon juice, Italian bread, anchovy fillets, parmigiano, Dijon, Worcestershire.

- Wash, dry, and chill romaine leaves, leaving the medium and small leaves whole.
- Make a garlic puree in salt and lemon juice.
- Separately, soak some chopped garlic in some olive oil for several days or hours, in advance.
- Cut some good Italian bread, that is a little stale, into large cubes and let them completely dry out.
- Prepare some anchovy fillets and mince them up or mash with a fork.
- Put the garlic puree, with its lemon juice, into a large bowl.
- Whisk in the anchovies, salt and pepper, some Dijon, and a shot of Worcestershire sauce.
- Whisk in some of the olive oil (that has had the garlic steeping in it), and an egg if you wish, until you have the dressing consistency you like.
- Dump in the leaves and toss well.
- Grate lots of parmigiano and toss well again.
- Salt and lots of fresh ground pepper.
- Heat the rest of the garlic-infused oil in a skillet and lightly brown the croutons.
- Then sprinkle them over the salad.

Marinated Salad Medley

Patrick: This is not so much a "salad" but a marinated compilation of flavorful ingredients designed to add to your leafy salad or to add that missing link to a special sandwich.

INGREDIENTS: Red onion sliced super thin, celery sliced super thin on a bias, carrot shaved with a peeler, fresh tomato sliced thin, garlic oil (3-4 cloves smashed garlic soaked in olive oil for a minimum of 24 hours), a dash of dried basil and oregano, red wine vinegar, salt, pepper.

- Mix together and let marinate a while before using.

Just Desserts — But Not Much

John: I debated, with myself for a change, whether to put a dessert lesson in the book. I do love desserts. It's just that a.) Eating them too often creates a weight problem and b.) as you can tell by now, I really don't have the patience for making them. The first point needs little explanation. The second point is that in general when it comes to baking (and face it, most great deserts are baked combinations of flour, yeast, baking powder, eggs, etc.) more exact measurements and procedure are required than when you're playing with a soup idea. Or experimenting on a new ravioli filling. Yes, I've baked and concocted some decent desserts, but I guess it's just not my main area of interest. As it turns out, my brother and I do most of the daily cooking in our homes, so taking the time to do desserts also gets a little too much. Anyway:

Fruit and Cheese

- If I cook a big meal – I mean a "special" feast for guests - then what I plan for dessert is a very simple one, and one that could easily become an every day thing. That is, fruit and cheese. Short of my wife's delectable berry pies, tart tatins, chocolate cakey-things, and so forth, my favorite, and as it turns out my grandchildren's favorite dessert, is a sliced fresh pear. Often this is accompanied by some room temperature cheese: say maybe a nice blue of some kind, or a nice fresh goat cheese.

  A quick digression here, but not really a "note". My grandchildren, ages 7 and 4, as of this writing, have their own expectations as to what they like to eat when visiting our house. Typically their appetizer, while I'm cooking dinner, is chunk after chunk of a fresh baguette with some nice unsalted butter slathered on. The favored main course is something in the pasta family, or "noodles". And dessert is a fresh pear or apple, sliced, or a tangerine. They know how to eat. Often I can get them to eat some romaine with a little olive oil and a touch of vinegar.

- Another basic Tuscan idea that I like a lot is fresh strawberries, cut in two, and soaked in a good red wine for several hours, in the refrigerator. I guess you could do the same with peaches and pears. Typically though, those two fruits are poached in wine, maybe with some sugar and/or other spices added.

- But fruit and cheese aside for the moment, often my wife and I simply break off a chunk of a fat bar of Belgian 72% dark chocolate, and munch on it while we sit down to watch a film after dinner.

I Have To Add These To This Truncated Lesson

- One very basic and traditional baked Tuscan style cake
- One very, very (and these days "tres chic") traditional "cookie", the famous "Biscotti di Prato".
- One a very basic rice pudding recipe, which I rarely make but is one of my favorite indulgences.
- Tapioca pudding (which I also rarely make, but which my wife adores).
- My rendition of a basic pastry crust which seems to work well with any type of recipe (dessert or otherwise) that requires a crust.

Corn Meal Cake

INGREDIENTS: Butter, cornmeal, flour, sugar, butter, dry white wine, fine unseasoned breadcrumbs, confectioners' sugar.

- Melt 6 tbls butter and let cool.
- Mix 1 cup of flour and ¾ cup of yellow corn meal together in a bowl.
- In another bowl mix ½ cup sugar and the butter together well.
- Add a pinch of saffron and an egg yolk to the sugar/butter, and mix.
- Slowly incorporate the flour/cornmeal into the egg mixture, along with 1 cup of dry white wine (a little at a time).
- Keep stirring the batter until it's very soft and uniform (about 10 minutes).
- Coat a loaf type pan with some butter and some very fine, unseasoned breadcrumbs.
- Bake in a 375F oven for about 1 hour and 20 minutes.
- If the top browns too much before the cake is done, put a piece of foil over it.
- When done, let rest out of the oven for 10 minutes then un-mold onto a platter.
- Sprinkle some confectioner's sugar over the top, and let rest until it's room temp.
- Slice as you would a loaf of bread into thick slices.

It's so simple and good as is. But dressing it up maybe with some honey, or fruit preserves is probably OK. Softly whipped heavy cream might taste great, too.

Syrup made out of boiling down some red wine and sugar is good for this, as well as for using on fresh fruit, such as strawberries, raspberries, or pears.

Biscotti di Prato

INGREDIENTS: Blanched almonds, un-blanched almonds, flour, eggs, sugar, saffron, salt, baking soda.

- Toast 2 ounces of blanched almonds and 6 ounces of un-blanched almonds on a cookie sheet for 15 minutes in a 375F oven.
- Remove from oven and mix all together.
- Grind a quarter of them into a very fine meal.
- Chop the remaining ¾ of the almonds into large chunks (3 – 4 pieces per almond).
- Make a mountain of 4 cups of flour on your work surface, and make a crater in the middle, like you were going to make pasta.
- Put 4 eggs and 2 cups of sugar into the crater and mix well with a fork.
- Add a pinch of saffron, a pinch of salt, and a teaspoon of baking soda, and mix.
- Slowly (again, like making pasta) incorporate flour into the crater mixture, ultimately scarping it up with a pastry scraper and working with your hands, then kneading it for several minutes until you have a very think dough.
- You do not need to necessarily use up all the flour.
- Divide the dough into 8 balls, all the same size.
- Roll the balls out into snakes about ¾ inch thick.
- Lay the snakes on a buttered, floured cookie sheet, or sheets, with ample room between them to allow for them to flatten out a little and spread.
- Brush the tops of the rolls with egg white.
- Bake at 375F for 18 – 20 minutes.
- Remove from oven (and turn the oven down to 275F).
- With a sharp knife, cut each flattened snake into ¾ inch slices, on a 45 degree angle.
- Spread the pieces out a little so they all have room to finish baking as separate biscuits.
- Put them into the 275F oven for about 30 – 45 minutes until they are very dry.
- Remove from oven and cool thoroughly. I usually do this on brown paper (like shopping bags).
- Let them rest in a paper back for a few days before you use them. They'll be good for a long time.

These aren't always served as a dessert with sweet wine such as "Vin Santo", after a dinner meal. Often they're used as an afternoon snack, or to serve to guests who have stopped by to chat.

For whatever the reason (I've forgotten now) I usually make these at Christmas time. But that's just me. They're not traditional holiday cookies.

Rice Pudding

My mother made rice pudding often, though I don't know her recipe. As I write this, Patrick is the keeper of the family's recipe box, since our mother is sliding (at age 93) into a state of mental confusion, bless her soul, and since our father died years ago.

Here is a recipe that works, though most "old-fashioned" recipes call for uncooked rice. When I make a meal that uses rice for some reason, I usually make more than I'll need, just to have leftover rice. Often I'll eat a little leftover rice for lunch with some hot Asian chili sauce. Just a quirk I have. Leftover rice is great for making fried rice, too.

INGREDIENTS: Cooked rice (basic medium grain white rice, but not instant, or a brown rice for a nuttier flavor and texture), eggs, sugar, vanilla, milk. Options are cinnamon, nutmeg, rums, raisins, etc. for the flavoring of your choice.

- Whisk together 4 eggs, ½ cup sugar (use some brown sugar if you want), 1 teaspoon of vanilla, and 2 cups of milk (I hate having to use exact measurements). Add raisins, cinnamon, cardamom, etc. as you wish.
- Crumble in the cooked cooled rice with your fingers so that there are no clumps, and mix.
- Pour into a buttered 8X8 baking dish.
- To better control the cooking temperature, place the dish in a larger baking dish containing water (but this isn't absolutely necessary). The point is to keep the cooking temperature steady at around 300F – 325F so the eggs don't curdle.
- Put into a pre-heated oven for about 45 minutes until done.
- Don't let it dry out too much. Custards, pies, etc. should just be barely set in the middle (still slightly wobbly).

Feel free to drizzle slightly whipped, or un-whipped, cream on each serving, if you want.

Tapioca Pudding

Like rice pudding, tapioca is something that people rarely make these days, but is one of the most satisfying desserts – ever! The only way to make this dessert is to start with real pearl tapioca (not instant), which are small little white balls the size of shotgun shot (or small bb's).

INGREDIENTS: Small pearl tapioca, water, milk (not fat-free), salt, eggs (separated), sugar, vanilla.

- Soak ½ cup tapioca in 1 cup water for 30 – 60 minutes.
- Add 2 ½ cups milk, ¼ teaspoon salt, and 2 lightly beaten egg yolks.
- Stir over heat until boiling then simmer very low for 10 – 15 minutes, stirring often.
- Beat 2 egg whites with ½ cup sugar until fairly stiff, but not over stiff.
- Fold about a cup of the tapioca into the whites, then fold that mixture back into the tapioca.
- Stir over low heat for a couple of minutes.
- Cool for 15 minutes, then stir in ½ teaspoon of vanilla (the real stuff not the fake).

Eat warm or cool. Like rice pudding, tapioca can be a medium for flavorings and toppings of your choice, if you wish.

Pastry Crust

As I said this works well for dessert pie crusts, savory tarts, or anything requiring a crust, in my opinion. I am not a baker, and a real baker may find fault with my statement and technique, but as far as I'm concerned, this works, and that's all that counts in my book (so to speak).

INGREDIENTS: All-purpose unbleached white flour, unsalted butter (and I mean butter), salt, egg yolk, ice water.

- Cut 8 tablespoons of cold butter into 2+ cups of flour and ½ teaspoon of salt with a pastry cutter until you have a mixture that has granules about the size of peas.
- With your fingers mix in an egg yolk until uniformly distributed among the granules.
- A tablespoon at a time add ice water, mixing with your finger tips, until you reach a consistency where the dough will just hold together in a ball, barely.
- Do not knead or over work the dough. You should be able to see little flakes of butter in the dough. You want to retain little independent flakes, or minute globs, of butter in the mixture so that the dough will turn out flaky.
- Press into a flat disk about 4-5 inches in diameter with your palms, wrap in plastic wrap and put in the refrigerator for at least an hour.
- When you're ready to make your pie, tart, or are otherwise ready to bake the crust (some recipes call for a partially baked crust, before fillings are added), roll out the dough on a lightly floured board. Avoid mixing in too much extra flour – only enough to keep the dough from sticking to the pin and the board. Use a flour impregnated pastry rolling cloth if you can find one, or use a flat weave dish towel, with flour rubbed into it.
- Roll out so that the dough extends at least an inch past the edges of a 8-9 inch pie or tart pan, after the sheet of dough has been tucked inside and lightly pressed to the inside edges.
- I do not trim the edges of the dough at this point but crimp and fold it up around the edges. I don't like a clean finished, uniformly crimped edge. It looks store-bought.
- If you need to partially pre-bake, cut a piece of parchment the size of the bottom of the pan and place it in the pan on top of the dough. Layer the parchment with some small pebbles all around, and bake at 375F for a bout 25 minutes.

I normally throw the stones back out into the driveway when I'm done.

Tart Tatin

Yes, it's a French dessert.

INGREDIENTS: Tart apples, sugar, pie dough, butter.

- Peel and thinly slice apples.
- Melt butter in heavy skillet.
- Add sugar and cook to a heavy syrup.
- Add apples, overlapping in a spiral.
- Simmer for several minutes.
- Put un-cooked pie dough on top and tuck in inside the edge of the pan.
- Put pan in a medium/hot oven until pastry is golden brown.
- Flip tart over onto a serving plate so apple side is up.

Serve with soft-whipped cream or crème fraiche.

Of course there's cheesecake, chocolate mousse and cakes, pear tarts, berry pies, and so forth. Maybe in another book that our wives write.

Menu Planning and Encore

Here is where we say goodbye and take a bow, if you're clapping that is, but not without saying a few last words on menus and other personal biases. As if you haven't heard enough already.

John: The way I think about menus is that the stuff you cook for a meal should look good on the table together and on your plate. I don't mean dressing up the food or plates with curly-cue squirts of some kind of red and green sauces shot out of a squeeze bottle, or large sprigs of curly parsley getting in the way of the food you intend to eat, or stacking things on top of one another to see how high you can pile your creations. Leave those devices to the restaurants that charge for the artwork.

What I mean is, the stuff on the plate should not only make sense together (nutritionally, seasonally, and gustatorially) , but should be balanced in texture and color.

So for instance, I might serve a golden yellow (colored from the acorn squash and egg yolks) squash and Arborio rice tart, some fresh spinach quickly wilted in warm olive oil (to keep it bright green) with toasted pignoli, and some pale cream-colored cooked cannellini with olive oil and fresh rosemary. Maybe too a room temperature salad of roasted red beets in a vinaigrette.

When it comes to menu planning, think of the simplest ideas which always work:

Monday: Soup (maybe a nice onion soup you make ahead on Sunday), salad, and bread.

Tuesday: Polenta with a porcini mushroom ragu, and braised broccolirab with olive oil and lemon juice.

Wednesday: Pizza with some greens as one of the toppings (like braised kale).

Thursday: Risotto with fresh peas – and salad of course.

Friday: A Summer stew (like "Cagoots") or in Winter a nice feisty pasta puttanesca.

Saturday: Do your slow braising or barbecuing thing, with slow-cooked polenta or fresh pasta, a squash tart, tart tatin, and salad.

Sunday: Make sauces, soups, pizza dough, etc. ahead for weekday meals. Go out for sushi or Indian food.

Christmas

- Get off the second-turkey-of-the-season bandwagon and roast a goose for a change. Stuff it with ground pork, chopped mushrooms, chopped goose liver, chopped olives, onion, garlic, cooked rice, and a crumbled bay leaf.

- Mashed turnips with lots of butter and pepper.

- Un-peeled chunks of a winter squash sautéed and braised in onion which has been sweated in rendered pancetta bits, with garlic, nutmeg, and bay – then baked in the oven with honey.

- A Provençal pureed fish soup with rouille.

- Leeks and fennel braised (in a covered casserole) in olive oil and bay.

- A tart tatin with soft whipped cream.

- A cheesecake made with very fresh goat cheese, lemon, eggs, and honey in a graham crust.

A Guest-Pleasing Menu

- Braised lamb shanks.
- Whole carrots braised with the shanks.
- Fresh wide (tagliatelle) egg noodles covered with the reduced braising liquid.
- A huge Caesar salad.
- Lots of bread for communal dunking (helps relieve the formality) into the sauce and wiping up salad dressing.
- A selection of cheeses, apples, and pears.
- Grand Marnier and some chunks of rich, dark chocolate.
- Fernet Branca as a degistivo.

John: I need to add here that when cooking a feast for a crowd, it's very, very important to select menu items carefully!

- First courses that can be cooked ahead and re-heated quickly (or served at room temp) are a big thumbs-up. Like for example pasta dishes that often taste even better after they've sat for a while.
- Main course things that cook by themselves without a lot of tending – like braised meats.
- Desserts that serve themselves – like cheeses and fresh fruit that diners cut up them selves (like pears and apples) to go with the chesse.
- Appetizers that can be bought or pre-made – like cured meats (salami, etc.), olives, salt cod spread.

Don't try to do too much, if any, cooking at the last minute or while you're trying to eat with your guests.

Plate each course at the stove, so the diners enjoy each course separately, and don't over-eat. Tell your guests what kind of wine to bring to complement what you're cooking. I think it's best to drink wines from the region that your menu is planned from. Don't tell guests to bring food! It's *your* meal!

Patrick: Sorry, the class is over. Go home to your family. It's up to you to come up with your own menus for everyday and holidays now. My final words are that unless you have lots of time to continually create something new, for the most part, you will have a modest to medium portfolio of dishes that you make on a regular basis with room to try or add things as time goes on. Your repertoire does not need to be huge - it only needs to be satisfying. Only bite off as much as you can chew – so to speak. Oh, and buy yourself a nice espresso machine. Forgot to mention that! Nothing is as relaxing and enjoyable in the hectic heat of the kitchen as a fresh espresso or cappuccino.

Afterword

John: If you enjoy cooking and eating as much as we do, you'll invent your own style, and forget all about us. That's our goal here in this little "school". When you've left the classroom, go home and make up your own interpretation of what you've seen here. It doesn't really matter what the "professore" *meant* or were *trying* to say – if they were trying to say *anything* at all. So long! Ciao! A bientot!

Patrick: La fortuna a te!

John: And remember, don't cook like my brother!

Patrick: And remember, don't cook like *my* brother!

Index

coriander *38*
corn
    grilled *146*
    in posole *96*
cumin *38*

D

desserts
    biscotti di Prato (hard almond cookies) *161*
    corn meal cake *160*
    fruit and cheese *159*
    pudding
        rice *162*
        tapioca *163*
duck
    braised legs *145*
    whole roasted *114*

E

eggs
    buying *149*
    fried *151*
    frittate *151*
    w/ green beans *153*
    hard-boiled *151*
    omelets *149*
    on a roll *153*
    poached *151*
eggplant
    grilled, in Napoleons *141*
    sautéed *141*

F

filled cookies *23*
fish
    brandade (salt cod dip) *125*
    buying *119*
    cleaning and filleting *21*
    fried
        w/ corn meal and salt pork *21*
        Venetian marinated *126*
        Provençal salt cod *126*
    grilled
        mackerel *121*
        salmon *122*
        tuna *122*
        halibut *122*
    shellfish
        buying *119*
        clams *127*

mussels *127*
oysters *127*
soup
    bouillabaisse *124*
    cacciucco *123*
    provençal *124*
focaccia (Italian flat bread) *52*
frittate (Italian omelets) *151*

G

garlic *34*
    in aioli *65*
    peeling *35*
    pureeing *35*
gnocchi *87*
goose (roasted) *116*
green beans
    stewed with milk and butter *22*
    w/eggs *153*

H

hamburgers *117*
hash (leftover beef pot roast) *24*
herbs *33*

J

jalopenos
    smoked (chipotles) *35*

L

lamb
    braised *108*
lasagna *80*
    al forno *82*
    vegetarian *83*
lettuce
    iceberg (salad) *25*
    mixed green w/ vinaigrette *155*
liver
    calves *20*

M

mackerel (grilled) *121*
meat
    bistecca alla Fiorentina (Tuscan grilled steak) *112*
    braising *105*